BEHIND THE LINES, NO. 2

Great Irish Sports Stories from *The42*, 2018

Behind the Lines

NO. 2

- - - - - - - - - - - - - - -

Great Irish Sports Stories
from *The42*, 2018

—

JOURNAL MEDIA

Journal Media Ltd
Golden Lane
Dublin 2, Ireland.
www.the42.ie

© Journal Media 2018
ISBN 978-1-9998774-1-5
Designed by www.grahamthew.com
Edited by Adrian Russell and Niall Kelly
Printed by ScandBook AB, Sweden
This book is typeset in 10.5pt on 15pt Sabon

The paper used in this book comes from the wood pulp of
managed forests. For every tree felled, at least one tree is planted,
thereby renewing natural resources.

5 4 3 2 1

CONTENTS

Around this time 12 months ago, we sat staring at the blank space reserved for the title of our debut anthology, crossing off each new suggestion as quickly as it came to us.

Muhammad Ali had the answer. He usually did.

'The fight is won or lost far away from witnesses,' Ali famously said, 'behind the lines, in the gym, and out there on the road, long before I dance under those lights.'

It is a quote that has always seemed to resonate with elite athletes, one which captures the long and lonely hours that are the price of a dream and inspires those who are chasing sporting immortality to persevere, uncelebrated and unseen. Growing up, Katie Taylor read those words every day, boxing's greatest passing on his wisdom to a little girl from Bray through a poster on her bedroom wall.

To us as journalists and writers, Ali's words carried a ring of truth in a different way. Much like Jimmy Breslin's inspired decision to write about a gravedigger at Arlington National Cemetery on the day of John F. Kennedy's funeral, or Bill Heinz's instinct to report the scene from the loser's dressing room, the best sports stories aren't the blow-by-blow accounts of the minute in which the winning goal was scored, or the detail of who supplied the final pass before the ball was pucked over the bar. Very often, the most vital and important experiences are the ones which play out at a distance from the pitch, the track, the ring and the court.

Behind the lines.

The stories within these pages hopefully reflect that belief.

Sport is their common canvas but they are stories of friendship and of families, of personal battles won and lost; stories told by generous subjects, willing to share and to allow the private to become public. It has been our privilege to meet and speak to people who have allowed us to come a little closer to their lives, their sport and, in turn, to society itself.

'If one person reads this and feels it helps them, that'd be a good thing,' Munster rugby legend Tony 'Mushy' Buckley told Paul Dollery when they spoke in May of this year. A few hours earlier, they had sat down in a café in Cork city to reflect on a life lived in the front row and to mark the anniversary of the province's 2008 Heineken Cup win. Neither of them anticipated a conversation that veered far from rucks and mauls as Buckley shared his experience of living with depression, anxiety and panic attacks for the first time.

For Buckley, sport — his memories of those many proud highs in red — can sometimes appear as a painful counterpoint to the fight he currently faces. For Willy O'Connor, the kitman with the Dublin Ladies football team, sport became his purpose, his path to rebuilding a life left devastated by a gambling addiction which started with a £1 bet at the age of 10. In the aftermath of the Blues Sisters' All-Ireland triumph, he met with Sinéad Farrell to tell his story.

The long-overdue need for conversations in this country around toxic masculinity, sex and power became even more urgent in the aftermath of the Belfast trial which saw Ulster Rugby duo Paddy Jackson and Stuart Olding acquitted on charges of rape. Australian journalist and author Anna Krien spoke with Paul Fennessy to explore the subjects which are the focus of her acclaimed and award-winning 2014 book, Night Games.

There are stories in this collection of heroic feats of mental and physical endurance, of prison cells and hospital wards, of communities bonded by unspeakable loss. There are stories too which might have only survived in the best oral tradition of the seanchaí, until chance and circumstance brought them to a wider audience in 2018. When a grainy video clip of a young Katie Taylor playing football for Newtown Juniors started to do the rounds online, it led us to Kenny Hammond who expertly filled the role of best supporting actor in recalling how he was on the receiving end of one of Taylor's crunching tackles that day. Pat Nolan was a more reluctant storyteller, far more at ease when praising his Limerick team-mates of the '70s and '80s than he was when discussing his own star-studded tale: big European nights against Real Madrid, swapping jerseys with Kevin Keegan, marking Diego Maradona.

Sometimes, sport just means more; that was the inescapable conclusion that Ryan Bailey found himself drawn to when he reflected on Ireland's historic and heroic odyssey at the Hockey World Cup. He spoke to Chloe Watkins and her family to recreate the incredible adventure which saw this team of amateurs, ranked sixteenth in the world and surviving on shoestring funding, take their incredible self-belief and infectious joy all the way to the World Cup final and a most unlikely silver medal.

'To see my sister go to a World Cup and not suffer the heartbreak that had been associated with this team for so long, but to go out and enjoy it and achieve what they achieved… we'll never forget that,' Chloe's brother Gareth told him.

That theme of family crops up time and again. In an award-nominated piece, Ryan delves deep into his own family's memories to recreate the tragically short career of his great-uncle, Liam Whelan, one of Manchester United's famous

Busby Babes who died in the Munich air disaster in 1958.

Family also links past and present for another of our writers, Eoin O'Callaghan, who traced the history behind an old football medal from 1926 which belonged to his grandfather, Daniel Dunlea. Daniel's exploits and achievements on the pitch never held more than a fleeting interest for Eoin, until May of this year when his mother passed away suddenly. Excavating the detail of his grandfather's sporting past for the first time allowed Eoin to find comfort and solace in a time of grief.

'I live in Toronto and on the plane journey back home, I stared into space a lot,' he wrote. 'I thought about the medal and its significance. It wasn't really about my grandfather anymore. It was about my Mum.'

Sometimes, sport just means more.

NIALL KELLY
Deputy Editor, The42

'I TOLD FERGIE TO SHOVE HIS MANCHESTER UNITED CONTRACT'

—

PAUL DOLLERY | 22 APRIL

'AN AMBITION HELD by nearly every young lad who has ever kicked a ball' was how the move was described on the front page of the Limerick Leader on 24 August 1985.

Just a few months after his 21st birthday, Joe Hanrahan from Ashbrook Gardens on the Ennis Road signed a two-year professional contract with one of the world's most famous football clubs; a club he had supported for as long as he could remember.

He was too young to recall how Manchester United became champions of Europe in 1968, but the FA Cup final victory over Bob Paisley's Liverpool in 1977 — when Hanrahan was 13 — remained vivid in his memory. Arthur Albiston, who played in that 2-1 win at Wembley, was about to become his team-mate.

It certainly was a 'fairytale story', as Limerick's local newspaper recorded it. Yet in spite of his childhood devotion to the club, moving to Manchester United wasn't quite the realisation of the dream for Joe Hanrahan. Having grown up a stone's throw from the Gaelic Grounds, his main sporting objective was to emulate his father.

The highlight of Michael Hanrahan's hurling career with Limerick came in 1958 when he won an All-Ireland minor medal. Joe was planning to follow in his dad's footsteps by representing his county at Croke Park, until life ultimately took him in a different direction.

'All-Ireland medals of any description are quite rare in Limerick, but dad has one — which he likes to remind us about,' he says. 'When I heard that United were interested in me, of course it was very exciting. But the main aim for me was to win an All-Ireland hurling medal with Limerick. That would have been unbelievable and the highlight above anything else, had it happened.'

Hanrahan did go on to play Gaelic football for Limerick at underage level, reaching a Munster Under-21 final thanks to a victory over Kerry in 1984. However, his ability with a football contributed to a much more significant achievement that year.

'If you weren't interested in talking about sport in our house, nobody would have spoken to you at all,' he laughs. 'Funnily enough, given how prevalent the game is in Limerick, the only thing we didn't do was play rugby.'

Peter, Joe's brother, was the League of Ireland's leading goalscorer when he won the title with Dundalk in 1991. Peter's son, Ben, is currently a member of the UCD side chasing promotion from the First Division. Another brother, Dave, also had a spell in the League of Ireland, while Gary represented Ireland at underage level.

The Hanrahan brothers made their names locally while playing for Vereker Clements. Joe's exploits with the club saw him recognised internationally. He captained the Ireland team that qualified for the 1982 European Youth Championship, but was unable to play in the tournament in Finland as it clashed with exams.

Prior to that, as he approached the end of his secondary school education, Hanrahan was on the radar of Dr Tony O'Neill at University College Dublin. After scoring for the Ireland youths in a game against Wales in Galway, O'Neill offered him a scholarship to study and play football at UCD. But 'The Doc' wasn't the only interested party.

Hanrahan explains: 'In the summer of 1981 after I did my Leaving Cert at Ardscoil Rís, my father came home one evening after meeting the head scout at Wolverhampton Wanderers. He basically said: 'Here's your choice — you can go to Wolves or take the scholarship in UCD. It's up to you.' That was the situation I was faced with.'

Although he was still only 17, Hanrahan's decision would ultimately prove to be pivotal in shaping his life. Understandably, young footballers find it difficult to resist the lure of an offer from a club in the top tier of English football. Hanrahan went down the road less travelled in order to put a safety net in place.

'You have to remember that this was 1981,' he says. 'Football in England was exciting, but it wasn't what we see nowadays where fellas are getting paid more in a few days than what some of the best players back then were getting in a year. It was an entirely different kettle of fish.

'I was also thinking that I'd be finished the degree when I was 20 anyway, so an opportunity to go to England might come again. That's why I decided to go to UCD and have that insurance policy in the back pocket.'

Making his League of Ireland debut as a 17-year-old left-sided attacker, Hanrahan describes his first couple of seasons as 'a rude awakening', as UCD constantly battled to stay away from the foot of the table. But the 1983-84 season represented a turning point.

Dr Tony O'Neill opted to break with tradition by signing experienced players who weren't UCD students, such as Paddy Dunning, Robbie Gaffney and goalkeeper Alan O'Neill. The change in policy brought about a top-six finish in the league, but the clearest signs of progress came in the FAI Cup.

They began with a 5-0 win over holders Sligo Rovers in a replay, in which Hanrahan scored twice. He then netted the winner in the semi-final against Waterford United, which set up a decider against a Shamrock Rovers side who had just won the first of four consecutive league titles.

After a goalless draw at Dalymount Park, a replay was required at Tolka Park five days later. Just before half-time, Hanrahan broke free down the left and tucked the ball inside Jody Byrne's far post to give UCD the lead. Jacko McDonagh equalised from the penalty spot for Rovers in the second half, and the sides were still level when the clock ticked past 90.

In the sixth minute of additional time, defender Ken O'Doherty — who was later signed by Crystal Palace — saw an opportunity to make amends. Having earlier missed a penalty that would have doubled their lead, O'Doherty went forward in the dying seconds and prodded the ball home from a Keith Dignam free-kick to seal a win which remains the greatest footballing triumph in UCD's history.

Rovers won the next three FAI Cups on the trot to supplement their dominance in the league. The missing piece in what would have been a four-in-a-row of doubles was that 2-1 defeat to UCD on Friday, 4 May 1984.

'We beat the best League of Ireland team I ever played against,' says Hanrahan. 'They were exceptional. I remember playing against them in a league match in Milltown before the FAI Cup final and they were superb. It was such a huge achievement for UCD. I was at a lunch recently and it was still being mentioned. It's nice to have been part of something like that.'

In spite of increasing interest from clubs on the other side of the Irish Sea, Hanrahan stayed with UCD for a fourth season, which saw him feature in another memorable occasion for the college. Their FAI Cup success sent them into the European Cup Winners' Cup. In the first round draw, they were paired with Everton.

The late Dermot Morgan of Father Ted fame is reputed to have put his support of UCD down to an aversion to crowds. To that end, he probably wouldn't have enjoyed the first leg against the English club, as an attendance of approximately 10,000 packed Tolka Park to see the likes of Neville Southall, Peter Reid, Kevin Sheedy and Graeme Sharp, all of whom had helped Everton to FA Cup success four months earlier with a 2-0 win over Watford.

The Everton side who came to Dublin in September 1984 is widely regarded as the greatest the club has ever produced. Nevertheless, UCD managed to hold them to a goalless draw at Tolka. Everton still progressed courtesy of Graeme Sharp's first-half strike at Goodison Park, but a 1-0 defeat over two legs to a team of that calibre was something UCD could afford to be immensely proud of.

That victory marked the first step on Everton's journey to winning the only piece of European silverware in their history. Their march to victory in the European Cup Winners' Cup final in May 1985 also included a 3-1 win over Bayern Munich. Eleven days before they overcame Rapid Vienna in the

6 I BEHIND THE LINES

decider, Howard Kendall's side were crowned champions of England with five league games to spare. Only a piece of Norman Whiteside brilliance for Manchester United prevented the Toffees from retaining the FA Cup too.

To add further perspective to the extent to which UCD punched above their weight, the most recent Anglo-Irish European tie at the time had occurred in the Uefa Cup a year earlier, when Drogheda United were beaten 14-0 on aggregate by Tottenham Hotspur.

'To be drawn against a team like Everton was absolutely amazing,' says Hanrahan. 'They were a really fantastic side. It was 0-0 at Tolka Park but it was 10 men behind the ball. We spent nearly the entire game in our own half. It was still a great result, especially as over two legs for the rest of the competition nobody else came within one goal of them.

'Even after the draw at Tolka Park, they were still expected to beat the sugar out of us at Goodison. It was a great experience. But did I think we ever had a chance of winning it over two legs? Not really. It was a traditional fighting performance from a League of Ireland team with the aim of getting a respectable result, which is what it was.'

Despite Hanrahan's assessment, Everton were only the width of the crossbar away from being eliminated. UCD struck the woodwork late in the second leg, which would have seen them through on away goals.

'It was the biggest scare we had en route to winning the Cup Winners' Cup that season,' Everton's Irish international Kevin Sheedy would later admit. Peter Reid explained in a 2007 interview: 'We beat them 1-0 at Goodison but in the last minute a lad called Joe Hanrahan had a chance and if he'd have stuck it in, we'd have been out.'

However, Hanrahan takes the opportunity to debunk that myth. 'I've seen that quote from Peter Reid and I think there has been a degree of embellishment. My memory of the game isn't perfect, but if we did hit the bar I'm fairly certain it wasn't me.'

In the summer of 1985, only a matter of weeks after Everton missed out on winning another FA Cup, Hanrahan was signed by the club who beat them 1-0 after extra-time at Wembley. After impressing manager Ron Atkinson while on trial, Manchester United paid UCD a reported fee of £30,000 to add Hanrahan to an Irish contingent that already included the likes of Paul McGrath, Kevin Moran and Frank Stapleton.

Upon his arrival in Manchester, the 21-year-old commerce graduate from Limerick shared a house with Mark Hughes, who was a key figure for United as they went undefeated in the first 15 games of the 1985-86 season. Hughes, who vacated the house the following summer to join Barcelona, scored 10 goals during that incredible run which looked set to propel the Red Devils to their first league title since 1967.

But the wheels gradually came off for United under 'Big Ron'. A dismal second half of the season killed their title challenge, and after winning just three of their first 13 games to begin the following season, Atkinson was replaced by Alex Ferguson.

All the while, Hanrahan was generally on the outside looking in. He played and scored regularly for the reserves, but a first-team breakthrough never materialised. The passing of time has allowed him to be candid in his assessment of why that was the case.

'The first thing I would say is that I had a great time there,' he remarks. 'It was literally like a busman's holiday. Really fantastic. Great fun, even though I didn't manage to break in.

'They brought me over as a centre-forward, which I never

saw myself as. I was more of a left-sided attacker, but not a striker like my brother Peter was. I was quick, I had a good left foot, a bit of skill and I could cross the ball. They were my strengths.

'In the reserves, you were always conscious of the fact that the first team was what it was all about and you were just waiting for a chance to get in. I'd like to think I got close a few times.

'I had a great pre-season in 1986. The reserves played a practice game against the first team, the reserves actually beat them and I scored the four goals. Ron Atkinson then took me on a pre-season tour to Holland with the first team but I got injured. That's one of the big things you find when you go into a fully professional set-up like that. The body takes time to adapt and you find that you pick up injuries because the body is being pushed.

'I was probably close enough at that stage. In a piece I read recently on The42, Liam O'Brien mentioned the game in which he was sent off against Southampton. I was part of the wider squad for that game, even though I wasn't actually on the bench.

'It was difficult. Because they saw me as a centre-forward, I was up against the likes of Frank Stapleton, Mark Hughes and Norman Whiteside. Big Ron bought Peter Davenport and Terry Gibson as well. There was a lot of competition.

'But the wider point I'd make is that until that stage, I had always played football for fun. It was only when I went to Manchester United that it ceased to be fun. It was a job first and foremost and you needed to treat it as such. Not everybody adapts.

'There are so many Irish players who go across to England with the requisite ability to succeed. But they're missing some other ingredient. Sometimes it comes down to that realisation that this isn't fun anymore. This is your living.

'Was I ever fully immersed in being a professional footballer at Manchester United? Was being a Manchester United player the be-all and end-all for me? Did I want it more than anything else in the world? If I was being honest with myself now, I would say probably not.

'The reality at the time was there was always an opportunity cost for me. When I was there, I was wondering what I was missing out on at home. I had a degree and I could have gotten into business while still playing football in the League of Ireland.

'After two years there, my hunger for it had probably diminished. You have to bear in mind too that today's financial rewards weren't there then. Not even remotely. There wasn't so much of a difference between what I earned there and what I could earn at home.'

Although Hanrahan hadn't made an impact at Old Trafford by the time his contract expired in the summer of 1987, Alex Ferguson was prepared to extend his deal to give him an opportunity to play his way into his plans. According to the player, however, the 'derisory' terms of the offer brought the pair into conflict.

Hanrahan says: 'I'm not afraid to speak my mind and nor is Fergie, as we now know. When he came in after Big Ron was sacked, I remember Gordon Strachan warning the rest of us because he had experience of playing under Fergie at Aberdeen. He said it was going to be a big change, and it was. It went from a very jovial kind of a place to being quite an austere place.

'He had a job on his hands but the reality was that a lot of young lads were frightened of him. Himself and Archie

Knox, his assistant, were rough in the way that they dealt with people. In some respects I had protection in the form of my education. If I wasn't happy, I was able to say 'good luck' and walk out the door. That's kind of what happened.

'When we spoke he said I needed to prove myself, like everybody else. At the end of the season he offered me an increase in my contract for one year, but the increase was rubbish, which I pointed out to him and which he didn't like. We had a row. I told Fergie to shove his Manchester United contract and he told me to get out of his office. The following day I flew to Shannon and never went back.'

While Hanrahan was no longer under contract with United, the club still had control of his registration. The Bosman ruling, which now allows out-of-contract footballers to move to a new club without the need for a transfer fee, hadn't yet come into existence.

Dermot Keely and Louis Kilcoyne, who were manager and owner at Shamrock Rovers respectively at the time, were keen to sign Hanrahan, but the manner of his departure from United made it a complicated process.

'This was pre-Bosman, so United weren't even allowing me to play in Ireland,' Hanrahan explains. 'Fergie rang me at home in Limerick and said, 'You'll never play again if you don't come back,' because they were trying to sell me at that stage.

'In fairness to the late Louis Kilcoyne and Dermot Keely, they contacted me and asked if I'd play with Rovers if they could sort something out. I said 'absolutely'. They eventually did, but the deal they came to was that if I ever left the jurisdiction again, United would get the transfer fee.'

Regarding his relationship with Ferguson, Hanrahan adds: 'For his first four years at United he didn't win a trophy and I kept telling people that I was right to have doubts about him. But I was very, very wrong. In fairness to him, he had a very difficult job when he arrived at United. I was probably too young to recognise that. I was only 22.

'You've got to be honest with yourself when you get an opportunity to reflect. I would say that having a job and playing football on the side probably suited my personality at that time a lot more than being a full-time professional footballer in England.

'If I was 22 today, it might be a different scenario. The rewards are just so incredible now that it might change the outlook. You've got to be getting paid as well as you can because it's such a short career.

'But with hindsight, I do agree with Fergie's assessment of me. To be fair to the man, he was right. It's very difficult to be honest with yourself when you're 22. I had plenty of ability, but did I have that inner desire that a Roy Keane had later on? No. Not to get to play with Manchester United at that level anyway.

'I always felt that my ability would be enough to bring me to the next stage, but in the professional ranks ability is only a component. There's an awful lot more to it than ability, which is what I'd say to any parent today coming to me with a child who's thinking about going after full-time football.

'There's an awful lot more to it than simply having a good left foot or whatever it might be. What's his head like? Is there a burning desire to do this? Can he adapt to a different lifestyle? It's easy for me to say that now with hindsight, but that's the reality.'

Hanrahan was a Shamrock Rovers player for the 1987-88 season, but perhaps most importantly from a professional point of view, the move allowed him to begin a long reign of employment in the financial sector in Dublin which continues to this day.

On the pitch, it was a difficult season for the Hoops as they sought to adjust to life at Tolka Park following their controversial departure from Milltown. After winning four league titles and three FAI Cups in the previous four campaigns, Rovers finished empty-handed in Hanrahan's only season with the club.

'Rovers had just moved from Milltown to Tolka,' he says. 'It had been an incredible period of success for the club but they were probably going over the other side of the mountain at that stage. There was a huge amount of discord with supporters wanting to keep the club in Milltown, so there were protests outside the ground and that type of thing. It was probably a very dark time in Shamrock Rovers' history.'

Hanrahan then moved on to play under Billy Hamilton with Limerick City, helping his hometown club to a third-place finish in the Premier Division. His form in Limerick attracted more attention from England, but the looming presence of Manchester United in any deal put paid to the prospect of another cross-channel transfer.

'On the quiet I went over to Sunderland for a few days. They were looking to sign me and I would have been happy to sign because I was happy with the terms. I wasn't itching to get back over to England or anything, but there was a slight sense of unfinished business. But Sunderland then saw that they'd have to negotiate with Manchester United, I wanted Limerick to get a few quid, and it fell into the sand from there.'

In 1990, Hanrahan headed north to join Jim McLaughlin's Derry City, where he won the League Cup in each of his two seasons with the club. The first of those finals was a 2-0 victory over Limerick, in which he scored one of the goals. 'I used to get dog's abuse whenever I played against Limerick. In fairness, it was in a good-natured way because they knew I was still one of them.'

He adds: 'Derry was a big commitment. There was a lot of travelling, going up and down from Dublin every weekend. I'd go up and train on a Saturday, stay in a hotel, play a game on Sunday and then come back down. So the social life was gone. It was tough but enjoyable.'

The 1992-93 season marked the beginning of a five-year spell at Dundalk, the highlight of which was a Premier Division medal that came in dramatic circumstances in 1995. On the final day of the season, leaders Derry City only needed to defeat lowly Athlone Town — who had already been condemned to a relegation play-off — to become champions.

However, with Derry held to a 1-1 draw at St Mel's Park, and Shelbourne — who were level on points with Dundalk — only securing a point at home to St Patrick's Athletic, Dundalk defied financial difficulties and a poor start to the season to win their ninth league title following a 2-0 win at home to Galway United.

Hanrahan, who had been reunited with Dermot Keely at Dundalk, says: 'The Dundalk years were fun. Dermot just did something to get it right. We came from absolutely nowhere to win that league. The club had been hanging on. I remember everyone on the pitch at Oriel Park, waiting for the news to come through that Derry had drawn in Athlone. One more goal and they would have been champions. Incredible scenes.

'There was a great camaraderie in that group, a camaraderie that I hadn't experienced since my days at UCD. That kind of completed it for me because my brother Peter won the league with Dundalk a few years earlier. It was great to be able to emulate what he had done.

'They say in Dundalk that Peter was a better player than me — and he thinks that himself anyway — so who am I to dispute that? It was a fabulous team, but unfortunately financial difficulties bedevilled Dundalk at that particular point. But I'll always have an affinity with Dundalk after winning the league with them — even if they like my brother more than me.'

Hanrahan knew that the end was on the horizon when he left Dundalk in 1997, but he played on for two more seasons in the League of Ireland — first with Bohemians, then Monaghan United. But the years were beginning to take a toll, to the extent that Joe Hanrahan became known as Joe Hamstrings due to his injury troubles.

'I was 35 by the time I finished and I had been on the go at that level since I was 17,' he says. 'If I was a car there would have been big mileage on me. I was getting injured a lot more often. I was just getting too old. The last few years were difficult. I was doing something I knew I wasn't able to do as well as I did 10 years earlier.

'As well as that, the attitude was catching up with me as much as anything else. My levels of commitment were being seriously tested at that particular time. I think my last game was an FAI Cup match against Cork City in Monaghan. I got the shepherd's hook at half-time and I knew then that it was game over.'

Having spent two years on the books at a club of Manchester United's stature, as well as winning every major honour in Irish football, he adds: 'I enjoyed the entire journey. I met so many brilliant people along the way, stayed fit, won a few medals and had lots of laughs with lots of very diverse people. I look back with absolutely no regrets.

'I suppose the education played an important role in that regard. Education is priceless, in my opinion. If you have your education, you'll always have leverage with whoever you're dealing with.

'If I did have one regret, it's that I was born in 1964 instead of 1994. If I was going to Manchester United now, the starting salary would be massively different. But that's hypothetical, of course, and I'm fortunate that I never had to consider any of that.

'I'm completely at peace because I can be honest about it. Did I have the ability to be a professional footballer in England? Yes. Maybe not necessarily with Manchester United, but for another club over there perhaps. But did I have the level of commitment that was required? Not enough. I was too distracted.

'If I was here [in Ireland], I would have been wondering if I should go over there. If I was there [in England], I'd have been thinking about coming back here. You can't be like that. You need to be all in to succeed at that level.

'I'll give the last word to Fergie on this. He was in Limerick a number of years ago for a Manchester United Supporters Club thing and he was asked about me by Alan English from the Limerick Leader. Fergie answered that they could never figure out what was going on in my head — whether I was in or out. That probably summed it up.'

If you ever happen to be on the hunt for financial advice in the Harcourt Street area of Dublin, there's a good chance you'll cross Joe Hanrahan's path. For the past 12 years he has been working for Investec, where he's currently heading up the retirement planning division. Yet even at the age of 54, he still hasn't quite given up on his childhood dream.

'It's 37 years since I left but I'm still very much a Limerick man,' he says. 'I still keep an eye on the League of Ireland and I'll always defend it, because I really enjoyed playing in it. But the hurling especially is still close to my heart, I have to admit.

'It's 1973 since Limerick won a senior All-Ireland. If you asked me for one sporting ambition I'd have from now on — even though at this stage I'll have to settle for watching instead of playing — it's to be in Croke Park to see Limerick win the All-Ireland.

'I was fortunate to have had some great experiences, but that's a dream I'll never give up on.'

HE COULD SEE HIS HOUSE FROM JAIL AND PLANNED HIS UFC TILT FROM A CARAVAN IN DUBLIN

—

GAVAN CASEY | 11 MARCH

YOU CAN'T BEAT a bit of small talk to punctuate the social debacle that is waiting for an unhurried card payment machine to process a transaction and spit out a receipt.

'Your UFC interview — it's not with Conor McGregor, is it?' asks the branch manager — Junaid, if memory serves — at Carphone Warehouse in Liffey Valley Shopping Centre, Dublin.

'He is a nice guy. He came in here to buy phones last year.

'He was trying to buy three phones: 'Gimme this one, gimme that one, and I'll have that one as well.'

'But I told him we can only do two phones per person. He said: 'No problem.'

'But he was trying to buy pay-as-you-go phones, so I told him: 'Why don't you switch to bill pay?'

'And he said: 'Look at me, man! Do I look like I need to be saving money?'

'I said: 'No, sir, but are you really walking into shops to top up your credit? It is not a look that really suits you.'

'And he said: 'My man, I like your style!' And he bought three bill-pay phones: two in his name — one for him, one for his girlfriend. And one in his mother's name, I believe.

'Lot of money!'

* * *

MADMAN

He's a gym-mate of 'The Notorious', but John Phillips doesn't live on a Conor McGregor budget. We meet in Starbucks: Paul Kimmage would puke but, to be honest, we're not on his budget either.

This is where the UFC middleweight tends to kick back on his way home from boxing training over at Paschal Collins' Celtic Warrior Gym in Corduff, a regular staple in his big-fight prep.

Phillips, 32, a boxer-turned-mixed martial artist whose propensity for first-round knockouts earned him his longstanding moniker 'The White Mike Tyson', has a fighter's handshake in that it's frightening to note how much he's holding back.

A former BAMMA world champion, he signed with the UFC in December 2016. Two-and-a-bit years on, he's in debt, he's yet to make his debut for the organisation, and he currently resides in a caravan outside John Kavanagh's Dublin home some 100 kilometres and a full Irish Sea away from his fiancée back in Swansea.

At least two of those things are set to change in the next six days, and the self-proclaimed 'right crazy Welsh bastard who's up for a row with any fucker' beams as he takes the first sip of what's either a latte or a flat white. Venti, vidi, vici.

'I could stay in a house — I could stay with one of the guys or I can stay in John [Kavanagh's] house,' he says, 'but I'd have too many luxuries then. It'd almost get a bit too easy, and I might get a little bit soft.

'I like the caravan because I've got to get annoyed about going to get water, I've got to get annoyed about sleeping on a little bed. And that adds to my training: I realise I'm sacrificing home comforts, I'm sacrificing being with my fiancée back home, I'm sacrificing being with my dogs. I'm looking at the guy on fight night, then, and I'm thinking, 'Alright, you fuck — *you* made me stay in a caravan for 20 weeks. I'm going to rip you in half.'

'The caravan was free, if you can imagine,' he laughs. 'It's got no comforts. You can just about eat in it and it can just about hold some water. My caravan is a 1982. She's a belter.

'It just about made the trip over here... I don't think it's going to make it back.

'As the great Welsh poet Dylan Thomas would say: 'I hold a beast, a little angel, and a madman in me.' And I think the madman is in the caravan. Don't come knocking!'

He's gone noseblind, he reckons, so not too many friends come knocking on The Belter's doors for a cuppa these days, but Phillips stresses that his current environs, however humble, have actually seen him move up in the world.

He used to stay in a regular van outside Kavanagh's Straight Blast Gym in Walkinstown.

'Listen, the van is great if you're spending the weekend down the countryside with your missus, but when you're in that van for three months? That'll fuck with your head,' he says with a puff of his cheeks. 'It's too much — it's like being in jail.'

It's been 18 months since John Phillips last earned a wage:

a toxic combination of injury and issues with visa applications have rendered his upcoming UFC debut one of the most delayed in the company's history.

The fact that he can even make it as far as next weekend, albeit barely, he attributes to his sponsors, Gavin Griffiths Recycling and Go Green Hydroponics — two Swansea-based businesses whom he politely asks be included in any written piece. He thanks them profusely.

His own job seems fairly thankless: Phillips, who has been fighting competitively for more than half his life, will only now begin to reap substantial financial reward for his toil.

And yet, were it not for a freak intervention in his youth — back when he moved with his father 20 minutes up the road from his original home in Penlan — he might have been worse off.

'I was about 13 or 14 at the time, and I had no friends there: I didn't know anyone, and I weren't a popular kid so I just wanted to hang around with anyone.

'I met a bunch of guys in my new school, and for some reason we decided one day that we were going to go into this car park to this old, derelict building that we thought was abandoned — it used to be a gymnastics centre. And we were going to smash the windows,' he explains with a sarcastic tinge of teen excitement.

'I'm grabbing rocks and I'm pelting windows, and a bunch of lads come out: Gwent ABC [Amateur Boxing Club] had moved into the old gymnastics centre unbeknown to us — we would never have gone near it if we knew it was a boxing club — and suddenly we're trapped in the car park, nowhere to go.'

The young vandals were duly hauled into the gym by its two chief trainers, Terry Grey and Paddy Simons — the latter from Derry. The ultimatum was simple: do a session with Terry

and Paddy or go home in a Paddywagon for the bollocking
of a lifetime.

'After a couple of rounds on the bags,' Phillips continues,
'the coaches say: 'Right, then, who's up for sparring?'' And
I didn't know what sparring was. I jump the gun and I go,
'Yeah, okay, I'll do some sparring.' My friends are like: 'Are
you fuckin' mad? Do you know what sparring is?'

'THEY EXPLAINED I'D have to go in and fight with someone,
and I'm thinking: 'Shit, I don't want to fight anyone.' But I
finally had friends, you know? I thought: 'I've got to win —
I've got to get in and prove myself as a tough guy.'

'I go in and spar this guy. I was 14 and he was 18, but he
was about the same size as me. But he was British champion
at the time. And he boxed my head off, he battered me. I could
see everyone watching, and I felt like I was going to cry — not
just from the embarrassment. I was getting badly hurt.

'I didn't want to show my new friends that I was hurt; I
didn't want to show the trainers I was hurt. So I thought,
'Right, when he hits me next, I can hit him.' Something in my
head told me that if he could touch me, I could touch him.

'As soon as I felt him touch me with — well, I don't know
what it was, but I assume it was a jab — I closed my eyes and
threw my left hand. I remember — 'Boom!' — hitting him
and thinking: 'Shit. He's going to batter me now. That was a
good shot.' So I covered up, eyes still closed, and I just heard
everyone gasp. And for what was only a second but seemed
like an eternity, I'm thinking: 'Why isn't he hitting me? Why
isn't he hitting me?'

'I opened my eyes and he was on the deck.'

A terrible beauty was born.

'I think I've probably tried that shot a hundred times in my life and only landed it once!' Phillips laughs.

'Paddy and Terry became like two other dads to me — or grandparents, even. When I went through some rough times, I could have gone to live with either of them. They always welcomed me. They're still at Gwent ABC today — they're like icons. I can't speak highly enough about them.'

He continued to box under Grey and Simons and, by his late teens, Phillips had accrued Welsh and British amateur titles in the ring as well as a reputation as a ferocious puncher — one which precedes him to this day.

His left hook was the hammer from hell with which he rained down upon adversaries who were more technically fluent, his propensity for violence at odds with the sweet science in its unpaid form.

That thunderlust, however, hampered his amateur boxing career.

He knocked out three opponents in the box-offs for the Commonwealths and qualified fair and square, but his final opponent — despite having been flattened by Swansea's Tyson — was deemed the better tournament boxer and selected ahead of him.

'I was pissed off with the boxing, obviously, then,' Phillips says.

He parted company with veteran trainers Grey and Simons when he outgrew them physically, teaming up with Mario Maccarinelli (father of former cruiserweight world champion Enzo) whom he describes as 'a maniac, but the best man I've ever met in my life'.

He enjoyed some of the best times of his life training in Maccarinelli Sr's gym, but amateur boxing was fast becoming too restrictive and points-orientated for the concrete-fisted wildman.

'I remember often thinking, 'If we were gladiators, I'd fucking kill this guy," he explains.

'I saw a fight DVD one day, and I didn't know what I was watching at the time but it was [UFC star] Wanderlei Silva. And I thought, 'Oh my God, this guy is a freak. I wouldn't mind having a go of this.'

'I had friends who told me it was a stupid idea, that no boxer could do MMA, and I kind of forgot about it. But then, out of the blue, Enzo [Maccarinelli] rings me up and says there are some cage fighters down in the gym looking for some sparring.'

Despite Phillips' initial trepidation due to his ignorance of mixed martial arts' ground game, Maccarinelli assured his gym-mate that the sparring in question would be boxing-only.

Phillips duly popped down for a tip-around.

'I knocked everyone out,' he says. 'Their promoter, who was there, was doing a show in Swansea called 'House of Pain [Fight Night 5]', and he said: 'You've got to come and fight on the card.' And I was like, 'Nah, mate, I'm a boxer.' But he was persistent, so I said I'd call his bluff.

'He said: 'I'll pay you anything to fight.' And I said: 'Alright, I want a thousand pound.' He said: 'I'll give you a thousand pound to fight.' And I thought: 'Aw, for fuck's sake, why didn't I say five?'

Phillips won his MMA debut by first-round knockout, but a sterner test was soon to follow in the shape of three-time British Under-21 champion 'Judo' Jim Wallhead, the defending 'House of Pain' titleholder, four of whose five pro wins had been quick.

'Man versus boy,' recalls Phillips. 'We knew nothing about each other, but as he's coming down [to the cage], apparently, someone pulled him aside and said: 'You're not going to beat this Phillips boy — he's the best boxer you'll ever fight.'

'So obviously he thinks, 'Well, I'm going to have to take him down.' Like, his name is Judo fucking Jim!'

Taken to the canvas with ease, Phillips suffered a broken nose and had his face rearranged by Wallhead's elbow, but he departed that Swansea cage with more profound scars than those which manifested themselves physically.

For the first time since childhood, he'd been on the wrong end of a bad hiding.

'I was so ashamed. I wouldn't go to the hospital for stitches in case people would see.

'I lived with my dad at the time, and I came back and I just stayed in my room — I kid you not — I didn't leave my house for three or four months. My friends would ring and I wouldn't answer. I used to hear my dad answer the phone downstairs and say, 'Oh, he won't come out: he's upstairs sulking.' And they'd visit, and my dad would shout up: 'John, Jason's here!' And I'd go: 'Tell him fuck off!''

Having vegetated in his bedroom for some 12 weeks he finally snapped out of his rut. And he was angry.

Defeat to Judo Jim was supposed to be Phillips' last outing in a cage: win, lose or draw, his boxing career was due to take precedence once more.

But defeat, and particularly one he perceived as being so humiliating, took a spanner to those plans.

Cognisant that he couldn't 'box off his back', he quite literally walked into a class with Wales' first ever Brazilian jiu-jitsu black belt, Chris Rees.

'I said: 'Chris, I want a jiu-jitsu fight. I'll fight anyone. I'll fight them tomorrow.'

'And he said: 'Well, I've never met you before, and you seem like a maniac. You need to learn jiu-jitsu.''

Phillips agreed to learn BJJ from the Welsh master, who volunteered to take to his corner for future MMA fights. But Rees's expertise lay in one martial art, not a mixture, and in any case he didn't have the time to assume the role of full-time trainer.

'I had a fight with Chris Fields — and that was actually the first time I encountered John [Kavanagh],' he says.

'In the second round, I broke my hand, and I went back to Chris Rees in my corner. I said: 'Chris, I've done my hand here.' And Chris said: 'What do you want me to do? Pull you out? I know you're not going to let me pull you out, so what are you moaning for?' And I said: 'Well something would be fucking nice, wouldn't it?'

'But I knew I'd have to try something different, because I couldn't throw my left hand or it would do further damage. And luckily, Chris [Fields] took me down.

'It was luck, really, but I thought: 'Hold on, I've got his arm in a triangle, here. I think it's on, anyway.' And I remembered what Chris [Rees] had taught me: when you've an arm in a triangle, you sit up — you don't sit back. I thought: 'Just squeeze.' And luckily enough I got the tap.

'John Kavanagh came up to me afterwards and said, you know: 'If you ever want to come to Ireland for a bit of training, just get in touch.' And I didn't know who he was,' Phillips laughs, 'so I was basically just like, 'Fuck off!''

Without a specialised MMA coach, however, Phillips soon fell behind his peers on the domestic scene and began to grow disillusioned and distracted.

He fought a couple more times under Rees but their partnership had reached its ceiling: both of them determined that it might be better if Phillips trained elsewhere. He still speaks glowingly of his former coach.

But following their split, 'The White Tyson' would draw another parallel with the former heavyweight boxing king after whom he was nicknamed.

'I fell out of love with the sport, I suppose,' says Phillips. 'And then I had a stint in jail.'

* * *

JAIL

Four years ago, John Phillips was arrested for attempted murder.

It was a crime he did not commit, and one for which he was never convicted: per British law, he was released from provisional detention after six months when it became clear that no case could be made against him.

That half-year in custody, though, was spent in Swansea Prison due to the severity of the alleged offence.

'It was a load of crap,' Phillips says. 'I was found not guilty but I had to do six months on remand. It was a fucking shit situation...'

His conspicuous discomfort in discussing the situation suddenly gives way to a wry smile.

'But I have some great memories from my time in jail,' he says.

Sorry?

'I was in Swansea Jail, and I could see my house from jail.

'As soon as I got there, the guy — kind of an assessor, who interviews you to see how much of a fucking idiot you are — was like, 'You're John Phillips.'

'And I'm like: 'Yeah.'

"Big house on the corner, yeah?"

'And I'm like, 'Yeah…'

'I'm getting a bit high and mighty — and a bit annoyed, to be honest — because he knows so much about me.

'He says: 'We'll bring you straight over to the 'D' wing — it's an open wing.' And I didn't have a clue what an open wing was, so I'm like: 'What are you trying to do, stitch me up or something?'

'And he's like: 'No, John. In an open wing, everyone has their cell open, everyone goes to work every day, but you can basically do what you want all day.'

'And I thought, 'Why is he doing this for me, like? This doesn't make sense.'

'Turns out the guy used to be my postman. But I didn't recognise him. That's how he knew me and my house.'

The former postman had at least spared him the induction period in which inmates must spend 23 hours a day in their cells learning about the workings of their new surroundings, although Phillips soon found himself 'bored shitless' in any case: all of his fellow 'D'-wing detainees had prison jobs and so the corridor was mostly empty during the day.

Stuart Phillips, one of two wardens in the prison and a combat sport enthusiast, alleviated that monotony somewhat: he granted the new detainee unlimited access to the gym.

His gesture was merely a sidebar to a cold dose of reality, however.

'He sat down beside me and he said: 'What do you want to be, John? Do you want to be just another name in this shithole? Do you want to tell everyone, 'Oh, yeah, I'm a tough guy in jail' and have no one give a fuck about you? You can get out of here and do something with your life.'

'And at the time I was quite annoyed, to be honest. I thought:

'Get the fuck away from me.'

'But it sunk in. It really did. If I ever see the guy again, I'd like to give him a big thank you, because it made a lot of sense what he said, and it stayed with me.'

The warden's was a worthwhile lesson, the prison's formal teachings less so.

Phillips' status in HM Prison Swansea saw him elevated to the top of his class before long, though, albeit in what initially struck as inauspicious circumstances.

'You go through education in jail,' Phillips says, 'and you're sitting in a classroom like a bunch of kids. We're sitting around a table, and I'm surrounded by junkies, lowlife scumbags.

'And all these fucking idiots are talking about which drugs they like, who they've robbed, how many times they've been in jail... And I'm looking at the woman who's supposed to be teaching us, and I'm like: 'Are we actually going to *do* anything today?'

'She says: 'Oh, you want to do something?'

'And I'm like: 'Yeah, well I haven't come over to listen to these useless fucking smackheads for the day.'

'She gave me some work to do, and I kid you not, it was like 'two plus two; spell 'cat'...' And I just said: 'Nah, I can't do this, I'm going.'

'She said: 'You can't go!' But I said: 'I'm fucking going.'

'But out of nowhere this screw [prison officer] then comes in — I've never seen him before in my life — but he says: 'PHILLIPS! Can I have a word with Phillips outside?' I'm thinking, 'Who the fuck is this guy?' And he takes me into this small, dark little room. I thought: 'What's going on here? Is this guy going to have a pop at me?'

'He says: 'Do you recognise me?' I said: 'No, should I?'

'He takes his glasses off, puts his face to my face and says: 'How about now?'

'I'm wracking my brain thinking, 'Fuck! Have I hit someone he knows? Have I slept with his wife?' I don't know what's going on. But I know that this guy is going to have a pop in a second, and I know that when he moves, I'm having him — I'm going to fucking nail him.

'And then he says: 'You train my son in the boxing club."

Phillips chuckles and sighs aloud as he recalls the moment which might have altered his life for the worse, but instead improved his detention exponentially.

'I told him: 'You idiot. I was going to hit you. How do you introduce yourself like that — in a jail — you fucking idiot?' We're having a laugh about it and he tells me I'm a madman, and I'm like, 'No, you're the fucking madman. I was about to go nuts."

But this plucky screw wasn't merely touching base with an old acquaintance for sentimental purposes: he had a plan.

The long-closed 'C' wing at Swansea Prison was to be reopened, its 20-or-so cells to remain completely drug-free. Phillips had been earmarked as the inmate best suited to keep an eye on its prospective inhabitants from within its basement-level confines.

He was told: 'You have on your wing who we want — and who we don't want, you tell them to go. You'll be segregated from the rest of the prison: when you go outside, it'll only be you guys. You can cook down there, you've got snooker tables, and it's really laid back.'

'And that was great,' he says. 'It was just a wing for me and my mates, basically. It didn't feel like jail. It was like having a training camp, or as if we were away on holiday.

'It was only at night when you lay down, you'd think: 'Hang on, I'm in jail here, and I could be looking at 15 years.'

'And it's crazy, like,' he adds. 'When you're released after six months it's: 'Ah, no harm done. We found out you're not guilty.' And I'm like: 'What do you mean? You've had me locked up in fucking jail for six months.'

'AND I KNEW I wasn't going to be found guilty, because it was a load of shit in the first place. But it was so annoying being in there because it meant losing my house and all that.'

This was a blow softened somewhat by the special someone who awaited Phillips on the outside. He evinces a rare shyness when he speaks of his now-fiancée, Kerrie — that is until he remembers the borderline farcical circumstances in which she learned of his detention.

'Actually, the day my girlfriend was coming down to live with me — she lived in Bristol — was the day I went to jail. So that was a test for our relationship!' he says only half-jokingly.

'She had no idea. I didn't even know it was happening. She rang me and she was on the way — she told me she was just coming over the Severn Bridge.

"Ah, okay,' I said. 'I've got to go into the station and give a statement, so if my phone's off don't worry — I won't be long. I'll be in and out.'

'I go in to give a statement, and they tell me: 'We're remanding you. We're sending you to jail.' And I'm like: 'Well, fuck.'

'Suddenly I'm looking at 15 years.

'I rang her from jail,' Phillips continues, 'and I said: 'Look, this is the situation. I shouldn't be in here, I'm probably going to be in here for six months, but I could be in here for 15 years, so... Just know there'll be no hard feelings,' and all that.

'She said: 'Whether it's six months or 15 years, I'll be here waiting.'

'That was massive for me,' says Phillips, who vowed to propose to Kerrie in Paris on his release — not that she believed him.

'And as soon as I got out we flew to Paris — and it sounds really cheesy, but I wanted to have this story that I'd be able to tell our kids when I'm older that I proposed to their mum on top of the Eiffel Tower.

'It's a funny story, actually: I wanted to do it in a little bit of a funny way, so I bought a packet of Haribo. I'd already bought a real ring, and I'd packed it in my hand luggage.

'And every time we go through customs, they search me. I've got that face. So when we get to the airport I'm already thinking: 'Fuck, I'm gonna get searched.' Like clockwork, they start going through my bag and I think, 'Fuck — she's going to see the ring. I've got to kick off, here.'

'So I kick off with one of the customs officers: 'YOU'RE ALWAYS HARASSING ME! I DEMAND TO BE SEARCHED IN A PRIVATE ROOM!' I'm going mad, so they drag me into a private room — I'm still shouting. We get in and straight away I'm like, 'Mate, I'm so, so sorry: I've got an engagement ring in my bag.'

'The guy, in fairness to him, burst out laughing and said: 'Best of luck.'

'I got out and my girlfriend was furious, understandably,' he laughs.

'But the fuckin' Haribo,' he says. 'She kept asking me if she could have some of the sweets on the plane. 'Just one or two.' And I'm like, 'No, I want to have them later.'

'We got to Paris, and we were only there for a couple of days, but the forecast was very bad — they were going to be shutting off the top of the Eiffel Tower for a while. So it meant I had to try and squeeze it all in on the day we arrived.

'We're in the queue for the Eiffel Tower and I open the little packet of sweets just to be ready. But I'm looking at the queue thinking: 'How am I going to make these sweets last?' She's like: 'Can I have a sweet?' And I'm like: 'Jesus... Have an egg!'

'We finally get up the top, right — loads of people around — and I've got the real ring in my hand, but I pull a Haribo ring out of the packet, and I say: 'How about this, then?'

'Everyone runs over thinking I'm proposing, and then they see the sweet so they think it's a joke. But as they're about to go away, I'm like, 'Ah, maybe not', and I put the sweet back in the bag and pull out the real ring: 'What about this one?'

'I remember she didn't know what to say; she started crying. And when she reached out to take the ring — the real ring — she dropped it: bounce, bounce, bounce, right to the edge!

'So she's still on probation now until we get married,' he says with a wink. 'No rush.'

* * *

BACK TO THE FUTURE

Having pieced back together his personal life, the Swansea puncher was reticent to return to fighting: he craved 'what's called a normal life.'

His 'brother' Mike — absolutely no relation — advised that he'd be off the wall to pack it in, but as Phillips explains: 'I didn't want it anymore. I'd lost that mojo: I didn't feel aggressive, I didn't feel angry, I didn't want to go through the hardship of training.

'Mike told me there was a competition coming up in

Glasgow,' he recalls. 'Winner takes all — 10 grand. And I said: 'I don't give a fuck, Mike. I wouldn't give a fuck if it was a hundred grand — I'm not interested.'

'I just felt, what would be the point? If I'm going to fight in this competition — then what?

'But there was still something missing. Everything was coming together life-wise, but I needed to do something. I needed a hobby.

'At the time we're building a new house — myself and the girlfriend.

'I've got no money but the roof trusses are coming in and the bill is 10 grand almost exactly. So I think: 'Right, I need 10 grand."

Sure enough, Mike got the call.

'We went up and I had a fucking nightmare making weight, because I was so overweight. I actually ended up having one of those... colographies? Some medical term, anyway.' (When asked if he's referring to a colon cleanse of some description he replies: 'Whatever it was, I don't want to remember it.')

We duly move on.

'Anyway, I won the tournament — knocked everyone out — and got myself the 10 grand. That's when John [Kavanagh] comes up to me again.

'I'd beaten one of his SBG guys [Charlie Ward] in the first round of the tournament — and I think if he'd beaten me, he would have won the tournament, and vice versa.

'And John says, 'Hey, you know, that offer still stands if you ever want to come to Dublin.'

'And again, I'm thinking: 'Fuck off."

Phillips returned to Swansea to put a roof over his head and leave MMA in his rear-view.

Cognisant of his atypically downtrodden demeanour, however, his fiancée eventually persuaded him to suss out Kavanagh's headquarters in Dublin.

He obliged more so out of curiosity than anything else, but on his arrival in Walkinstown, immediately became besotted with the SBG setup as well as Kavanagh himself, who by then was renowned as having helped steer Conor McGregor to the pinnacle of the UFC's featherweight division.

It dawned on Phillips that if he was capable of taking his own MMA career to another level, Kavanagh's Dublin hub would provide a springboard.

It wasn't long before he had 'The Talk' with his prospective trainer: 'What do you want from this?'

The question alone rocked him, for he'd never previously arrived at a concrete conclusion.

But Kavanagh told him in no uncertain terms: train at SBG for six months and he would become a world champion under one promotional banner or another; put in the work and he would be signed by the UFC.

Phillips took some convincing but slowly came around to Kavanagh's way of thinking.

Months later, an epiphany on the escalator in Liffey Valley on his way to lunch — in which it finally dawned on him that he was indeed the beast Kavanagh had told him he was — resonated to the point that he fought fellow knockout artist Cheick Kone for a BAMMA title while effectively operating off one leg.

On that occasion it was Kavanagh who took some convincing not to pull the plug on his injured fighter's championship fight at Dublin's 3Arena. Both his patience and Phillips' stubbornness were vindicated, however.

'I knocked Kone out in 60 seconds, or whatever it was,' smiles the Welshman.

But even with a banjaxed knee, the fight transpired to be the easy part; claiming the belt — his belt — proved more difficult.

'Every time I come over here, I'm always stopped by the customs at the ferry in Pembroke,' Phillips says. 'They'll ask: 'What are you doing in Ireland?' I tell them I'm going over to train, that I'm a fighter, that I'm going to be fighting for world titles soon.

'The lads working at customs say to me: 'Oh, when's the fight, when's the fight?' And I had it in my head that I can't go back to Wales on the boat and tell these customs guys that I've lost. I swear, man, I was thinking about this before the fight.

'So when I won the fight, I got the belt. The organisers come to me and say: 'Right, John, we've got to have the belt back. We've only got one belt for all the weights.'

'I'm like: 'Are you fucking kidding me? I'm not giving the belt back. I want to take it to show the customs guys — and the people at home.'

"Listen to me now,' I said. 'You seen what happened to that guy [Kone], and the same will happen to anyone who tries to take it off me. If you want to take it out of my wage, do, but it's more sentimental than money.'

'And one of the organisers says: 'Right, we're going to get the [BAMMA] owner now. There's going to be trouble, John. We've got to have that belt back.'

'So the owner comes down, he says: 'What's the problem, here?' Your man goes: 'JOHN! HE WON'T GIVE THE BELT BACK!' And the owner looks around and goes: 'Well, there's no one here who can fucking take it off him, so let him keep it.'

'I wouldn't mind, but the next day, I'm driving down to Rosslare, and when I get there, there's no customs. And when

I get off at the other side, in Wales, there's no customs there either. I was gutted, for fuck's sake.'

* * *

THE UFC

John Phillips compares his UFC career to packing the car for holidays, driving to the airport with one's family and missing the flight.

'You're relying on this money to live,' he says. 'And to tell you the truth, I get so pissed off sometimes that yeah, I think: 'Do I really want this? Do I really need to be putting myself in debt for this?''

Phillips, for whom injury and visa debacles have put paid to his getting off the mark under the UFC banner and, therefore, his ability to get paid, remains incredulous at how it has all played since he signed with the organisation in December 2016.

He'd be the first to admit he's been the architect of his own downfall on occasion: there was that time when he caused a minor security incident at the US Embassy in London, for example.

But take in isolation the circumstances which enveloped his original debut, scheduled for Denver, as evidence of dumb luck: he trained for high-altitude; his visa application didn't go through; the fight got cancelled; he returned to Wales dejected and, while walking his dog on the beach, nonchalantly threw a stick into the sea and blew out his knee.

This was an omnishambles which cost him over half a year, as well as a potentially significant paycheque.

His UFC bow was then rescheduled for California eight months later, but Phillips had immediate concerns given the visa impediment which had put a kibosh on Denver earlier in the year.

'I thought: 'Shit, this isn't going to be good," he says. 'I knew I had to train for the fight, but I also knew the likelihood was that I wouldn't be allowed to go.

'I knew I was setting myself up for a fall: I'd have to explain to everyone — again — that the reason it wasn't going to happen was because I couldn't get a visa.

'And the annoying thing is I've been to America 10 times — literally — and now that I want to go to fight there and pay taxes there, there's a big problem.

'I wasn't convicted when I was in jail, so there's genuinely nothing on my record about it,' he continues.

'When I went to apply the first time, it was in Dublin. I get up to the counter, and he's a little Hitler of a guy. And you can hear everyone up there: 'I'm a drummer for U2' — crazy stuff. And he asks me what I do. 'I fight for the UFC.'

"U-F-What?' he says to me. 'Oh, eh, I fight for a professional fighting organisation. I need to get to America to fight over there. I've been to America before.' And he asked me why I came to the American embassy in Dublin instead of Wales, and I explained that there is no embassy in Wales.

'He ends up failing me for 'having no home ties': Section 2.1.4 [B], or something. And I *have* home ties. I've got a mortgage, I've got a fiancée — who was pregnant at the time. I had home ties if he had just asked.'

'I told John [Kavanagh], who couldn't believe it, so we set up another meeting with the same embassy guy. John told me: 'Look, sometimes these visa guys get a little bit funny, but they all love Conor' — as in McGregor — 'so mention Conor's name, you'll get the stamp, and you'll be straight through.' I didn't want to do that because I didn't even know Conor at the time, but I could feel the interview was going badly, so with some hesitation, I go: 'Ugh... I train with Conor McGregor."

No joy.

And so Phillips tried the London embassy per this officer's advice — first to apply for a holiday visa for a friend's stag-do in Las Vegas, and later for a work visa appointment scheduled and paid for by the UFC.

Despite having been to Vegas a year prior as a tourist, his holiday visa never came through: he missed his friend's stag-do and was left out-of-pocket for flights and accommodation.

Still, he felt the work visa would on this occasion prove easier to attain due to the UFC's involvement in the process.

But when he returned to the embassy in London, he just so happened to be dealt the very same character with whom he had lodged his failed holiday visa application.

'Oh, the fighter. You're back.'

'He told me I seemed desperate to go to America,' says Phillips, 'and I explained to him that of course I was: I needed to get paid like anybody else. He asked me all these questions about the fight game — the ins and outs of a duck's arse, basically — and eventually asked me where I'd be fighting.

'My mind drew a blank.

'I'm like: 'Ah, ehhh... emmm...' — I couldn't fucking think of California!

'Failed. Section 2.1.4. [B] — again! And I said to him: 'Listen, mate, it's cost a lot for me to get over here, and I know what Section 2.1.4. [B] means. I do have home ties. Mortgage, business, fiancée, family.

'He's there: 'You've gotta go.'

'I said to him: 'I don't mean to be rude, but you're making

a mistake. I've been to America 10 times.'

"You've got to go.'

'And there's a guy on one shoulder saying to me: 'Stay calm, you're going to fuck it up for yourself.' And there's a voice on my other shoulder saying: 'Smash the window and grab hold of him."

The sane voice won out to begin with, but when Phillips's request to speak to a superior was curtly rebuffed, the maniacal voice opposite won out:

'I said something along the lines of: 'Listen to me you little cunt. You're an arsehole, and you're lucky there's a pane of glass between us or I'd rip your fucking head off. Now go and get your manager you prick."

He was duly marched out of the building by a pair of armed security guards.

'I come out and my friends are waiting for me outside, and they're like: 'How did it go?' And I'm like: 'How does it look like it fucking went? Look at these two fuckers next to me!' The UFC rang me up: 'How did the interview go, John?' I said: 'Well, to put it nicely, I got escorted out by two armed guards.'

'They said: 'Seriously?' And I'm like: 'No, yeah, seriously."

Phillips has been back to the London embassy since, where he was recently informed that his specific case is 'in administration' — deferred to some higher power — but this process may take six months or longer. Sparing no colour, he relays his opinion that the embassy might have informed him of this latest snag via email rather than have him return in person.

He remains hopeful of a transatlantic scrap later this year, but in the meantime will finally earn a paycheque via a long-awaited UFC curtain-raiser next Saturday. His opponent is 9-4 middleweight Charles Byrd, himself a UFC debutant. The venue? London, naturally.

He can smell the paycheque, but he knows better by now than to get too excited.

'I've fallen off the path a few times, but I'm fucking back on it now and I've got one thing in sight,' he says.

As he gets up to head back to his caravan, Phillips mentions how he hopes the Irish MMA public get behind him as they have done their own UFC breakouts.

His father recently revealed to him that his grandmother hailed from these parts. Phillips, excited to discover he had Irish blood in him, visited an ancestry website in search of further Irish connections.

The 50-odd-euro sign-up fee vanquished his curiosity, if only temporarily.

He promises that if he picks up the knockout bonus on Paddy's Day, we'll hear plenty more about Mrs O'Brien and her descendants.

One suspects we'll hear plenty more from John Phillips in any case.

THREE

NIGHT GAMES: GETTING TO THE HEART OF TOXIC MASCULINITY IN SPORT

—

PAUL FENNESSY | 20 APRIL

'A little appalled, my friend looked me in the eye. 'Those men had all the power,' she said. 'She was in a strange house, in a bedroom with most of her clothes off, and a bunch of guys she does not know came in expecting to fuck her. I mean, did they even prepare themselves for the possibility of her saying no?'
– NIGHT GAMES, 2014

FOR ANYONE WHO has read Anna Krien's 'Night Games', some of the behaviour of the accused in the recent Belfast rape trial will seem depressingly familiar.

The book, which was originally published in 2014 and subsequently won the William Hill Sports Book of the Year award, is essential reading for anyone seeking a better understanding of toxic masculinity in sport.

First and foremost, it focuses on the rape trial and eventual acquittal of a young minor-league Australian Rules footballer.

In order to protect their anonymity, the names of the defendant and complainant are changed.

An individual who is referred to as 'Justin Dyer' is charged with the rape of 'Sarah Wesley', after what he claimed was consensual sex in an alleyway in Melbourne the night/morning after the 2010 Australian Football League Grand Final.

As she reports on the case, Krien is granted access to the defendant and his family, but never meets the anonymous complainant (whose evidence was given in closed court and could not be reported) — an issue she admits is problematic.

Before the incident involving Dyer occurred, Wesley told a friend she was raped in a bedroom at a party, with at least two high-profile Collingwood footballers suspected of committing the act. The vast power of the team quickly becomes apparent, however, and the investigation of the two full-time professionals is dropped.

Dyer, meanwhile, becomes the central accused figure, having initially been told he was a witness. The case was consequently complicated by the fact that the incident in the bedroom leading up to the alleged rape in the alleyway is not allowed to be discussed in court.

In addition to an account of this particular court case, the book also serves as a wider exploration into the dark side of sport and a comprehensive look at the underlying misogyny that undermines its more positive aspects.

Krien highlights a number of horrific and shocking stories involving sporting figures and their treatment of women, which range from deeply unsavoury to blatantly criminal — over 20 accusations of sexual assault had been made against Australian sports personalities in the decade leading up to the book's publication, while the practice of 'gangbangs', the macho culture of humiliation, slut shaming and the dismissive attitudes of authority figures are all recurring motifs.

In short, 'Night Games' explores a world where women are callously used as props in male-bonding exercises. It is not anti-sport, Krien is keen to point out, but a work that rails against the worst excesses of jock culture.

The book is also an invaluable educational tool, full of razor-sharp insights and illustrations of the deep complexity that often characterises rape cases and how they are adjudicated.

Some of the common clichés and conventional wisdom about issues such as consent are also thoughtfully deconstructed. Consider, for example, the following passage: 'For all the good intentions of the feminist slogan 'no means no', the resulting awareness has been too simplified and the true meaning of consent has fallen by the wayside. After all, by the logic of 'no means no', surely 'yes means yes'? But people agree to do things all the time without an understanding of what they are undertaking. True consent relies on three factors: a capacity to say yes, a knowledge of what exactly one is saying yes to, and that the decision to say yes is an independent one, free of threat.'

Krien speaks to *The42* about her reporting on the Australian 'Night Games' trial in the aftermath of the high-profile Belfast case in early 2018. At the end of a nine-week trial which dominated headlines, all four defendants — Ireland and Ulster rugby players Paddy Jackson and Stuart Olding, and their friends Blane McIlroy and Rory Harrison — were found not guilty on all charges.

Jackson and Olding were both acquitted on individual charges of raping the same woman at a Belfast house in June 2016, while Jackson was also acquitted on a further charge of sexual assault. McIlroy was acquitted on a charge of exposure, while Harrison was acquitted on charges of perverting the course of justice and of withholding information.

Discussing her decision to spotlight the Australian case at the centre of the book, Krien says:

'There were quite a few stories going around and quite a lot of allegations of hush money being paid to females by football clubs [in Australia] to shut up and disappear, basically, when it came to allegations of sexual assault against certain footballers,' she says.

'I would be pretty sure there's a similar culture in Ireland — there are boys that can do no wrong — and it was sort of an inevitable book to write in that sense. I'm kind of surprised that it hadn't been written yet in that way. It's a locker-room mentality, which feeds into a much broader culture of influence and power and a sense of entitlement.

'In AFL Football, it gets a lot of government funding and the taxpayers put in a lot of money without really knowing. Therefore, I think it has a responsibility that it didn't seem to be meeting when it comes to respect and valuing women, and not only that, but also [it was] arresting the development of these young men, basically allowing them to be juveniles right into their old age. So it was a kind of no-brainer book in a way.'

Covering a high-profile case surrounding allegations of rape and spending significant amounts of time with the accused's family would be an unenviable task even for the mentally toughest of journalists and Krien admits to finding the process of documenting her experiences over the course of a 288-page book somewhat wearying.

'I guess it was emotionally draining, because you have to look at yourself and your own experiences as a female and particularly as a young female. And whether you had brushes with sportsmen or all those kind of things growing up, a lot of the stories that you hear are familiar and you become almost numb to them and that's the shocking thing in a way. As a woman, you become so accepting of certain behaviours.

'The case that I covered was quite eye-opening in terms of watching a criminal trial and seeing how much the jurors weren't allowed to know and also seeing the impossibility of it, the impossibility of proving rape basically, of proving consent or non-consent and the ridiculous ideas that people have about what rape is and what rape looks like.

'And the fact that it would be impossible to know what it's like until you've experienced the moment of powerlessness and seeing how you haven't reacted in the way you would like yourself to have reacted. So I think that was really revealing when I saw what happened to a rape allegation in court [in Australia].'

In theory, journalists are expected to remain cool and detached no matter the subject they cover. Reporting that could in any way be construed as biased or emotional at best can seriously harm the reputation of the individual in question. Yet sometimes taking this cerebral approach is easier said than done, particularly when it comes to such an emotive issue.

'Objectivity is always something you could strive for,' Krien explains. 'But in a way I found it difficult, because I found myself coming quite close to the defendant's family and wasn't allowed access to the complainant.

'That was a really tricky situation, because I felt immense sympathy for the young man. In a way, I think he behaved incredibly badly and I also think he'd been left out to dry by the football world, while others had been coddled and looked after by their [lawyers]. So I wasn't detached, I was very much attuned to everyone's humanity in that sense.'

Of 'Justin', the figure at the centre of the court case, Krien adds: 'He was quiet, he bizarrely struck me as quite gentle and he struck me as incredibly immature as most footballers of that ilk strike me.

'When they graduate from high school, for most of their peers, their world expands, whereas with these footballers, their world constricts — they don't meet new people, they don't go to university, they don't cross paths with a range of diverse opinion. They go into the club.'

Krien chose to structure 'Night Games' in a non-chronological fashion. The 'not guilty' verdict is highlighted at the outset, as if it is almost incidental to the larger issue. Instead, the trial serves as merely the latest example of the problems inherent in Aussie Rules football. While recounting the matter at hand, the author simultaneously and seamlessly veers through this awful history of the dreadful behaviour demonstrated by countless high-profile figures in relation to women and the deep-rooted misogyny that seems to be an inveterate feature of sport.

By effectively pushing it to the side, Krien's intention was also to highlight the inadequacies of the law in cases such as the one documented.

'I started with the 'not guilty' verdict immediately because I wanted to make the point, that court is not where progress is made, it's just where things end up,' she recalls. 'They're kind of dead ends in a way, they don't work when it comes to sexual assault of this nature and so I wanted to really just start from the verdict and work back from that, as opposed to building up the suspense as if court was going to deliver any kind of justice, which it never was going to.

'The idea that if you get a 'not guilty' verdict, then you're clean or you're vindicated or something. And the girl was what? Confused? Or lying? It just doesn't capture the complexity of the issues.'

Despite the author's noble intentions and abundance of praise she received when her critically acclaimed work was finally published, perhaps inevitably, Krien encountered plenty of antipathy while writing the book and even thereafter.

She was treated with deep suspicion and even outright hostility on occasion, as perceived 'outsiders' who condemn the practices of particular sports invariably tend to be. The fact that she was not an out-and-out sports journalist compounded this ill feeling, but also gave Krien a greater sense of freedom and distance in writing the book. Had someone already deeply embedded within the industry tried to write 'Night Games', it is doubtful that the result would have been nearly as effective.

'There was definitely a sense of trampling on territory that I didn't belong in. The usual dumb [stuff]: 'What would she know?' That's sort of to be expected. I don't know if it matters what you write about, you're always going to get dumb comments like that.

'There was blowback from the elite footballing world, there was blowback from feminists because I did have empathy for the accused, I did explore his version of the story and I did consider those kind of ideas of sex and regrettable sex and also those things that people get angry about — you shouldn't question someone's opinion or someone's declaration of rape, I analysed all those things.

'I think one of the rewarding moments was when I was contacted by several community football coaches who said that they'd given the book to their Under-15s, their boys, and that was when I was like, 'That's exactly what I want.'

'What do I care about a pseudo-academic sitting in a stuffy university? I need the boys to be reading this — they need to learn what the lines are and they need to learn how to stand up for their female [counterparts] and to have respectful friend- ships with females and to not be cut off and to [feel] this sense of entitlement just because of the way they play with a ball.'

But despite the situation they are in and the pedestal they are often put upon by society, Krien does not necessarily agree that sports stars are more prone to this type of egregious behaviour than the average person.

'I think it's got to do with this team thing — you don't see it with tennis players. People cross the line and there could always be other examples, this idea of spit roasting and everyone getting a go at it and just walking into a room unannounced, already unbuckling your pants without even considering how that might look from the female's perspective, it's not as if she can stand up and say, 'Actually, I'm not really interested.'

'There's this expectation that if she was not into it, she'd be able to extricate herself from that situation. It seems to be a big team football kind of thing and I guess it's the poison and the magic — they're so close to each other and they know where [their team-mates] are on the field. They can throw the ball without looking because they know their team-mates are going to be there. But when you take that out — off the field — into the night, they're still not really thinking of anyone else but each other, and that seems to be a real team thing, and it's really problematic.'

And while these issues are more publicised than ever, they are not strictly a modern phenomenon. On the contrary, there is overwhelming evidence to suggest they have been deeply ingrained in sport for decades. Krien does feel, however, that the problems have intensified in more recent times.

And of course, the behaviours in question also transcend sport to a degree and highlight deeper social issues, such as the chasm in how many men and women perceive issues like rape and consent.

'When it comes to rape, I think we're still obsessed with women in the sense that we're only obsessed with educating women how to not get raped and educating women what they should and shouldn't do with their body and what they should and shouldn't do with their face and we're not talking to the boys at all and that's really sad, because we're neglecting boys. We're not giving them responsibility, we're not giving them a sense of duty as to how they should treat their fellow person.'

For all their distressing aspects, perhaps the only positive ramification of these high-profile rape cases is that they force the media and people in general to an extent to confront the issues and start having serious conversations about consent et cetera.

Another common theme of the book, and one that is perhaps influenced by some people's distorted views of sex, is the men involved claiming they thought the women were 'up for it'. Krien believes there are instances where the accused genuinely have mistakenly believed it to be the case.

'I have seen accused young men completely bewildered with the situation they found themselves in, but stupidly immature, ill-advised and surrounded by idiots, as in the club.

'Who are their mentors? These dyed-in-the-wool arseholes basically, who just believe in nothing but the entitlement of the footballer. So again, I kind of felt like the anger could easily be redirected. Not that the accused would have no responsibility or anything like that, but I think the wider club and the wider culture should bear a lot of the brunt as well.'

One of the most tragic elements of 'Night Games' is that it highlights precisely why victims are often so reluctant to come forward in the first place. A 2012 article in *The Independent* stated: 'One in 10 women has been raped, and more than a third subjected to sexual assault, according to a major survey, which also highlights just how frightened women are of not being believed. More than 80% of the 1,600 respondents said they did not report their assault to the police, while 29% said they told nobody — not even a friend or family member — of their ordeal.'

Facing questioning in the course of a trial is an incredibly difficult scenario at the best of times, and particularly when it relates to such a sensitive subject. One particular talking point in the Belfast trial was the manner in which the complainant was interrogated by the defendants' legal teams. But while the intense media scrutiny of the trial prompted many observers to condemn these practices, they were hardly a departure from normal standards. According to a report in the Irish Times, three in 10 rape trials involve questions about the complainant's sexual history.

'Not in the particular trial I covered [in Australia] but in another trial, the questioning of the complainant was appalling down to what kind of undies she was wearing and how short her skirt was,' Krien recalls.

'In a sense, you could say it was just a defence lawyer doing his job and his job was to paint the picture of the 'typical slut' and just play to these ridiculous stereotypes we have of women: 'There are good women and there are bad women, and this one happens to be a bad one.'

'It was troubling in the sense that I left court having very little faith in it.'

Accordingly, in the wake of the Belfast trial and acquittals, wider discussions have been taking place in Ireland. People in the media and elsewhere have lamented the struggles of boys and men to understand some basic tenets of consent. There has been talk of the topic being introduced into Irish schools and in some instances, these initiatives are already under way.

'Consent is clearly an important issue to discuss,' Krien adds. 'I think there also has to be an awareness of one's presence in a sense and what that presence might do to someone else and to be able to picture how another person might feel in a situation. That's a schoolyard thing. It happens in the playground all the time. You see the kids. They suddenly all decide to gang up on one kid. They need to read those signs and read them in more complex scenarios.

'I think a lot of young men really don't see it like that, they walk into a bedroom, there's a couple in there and some kind of weird porn music playing in their head. They have no concept of the 19-year-old who's looking at it through a completely different eye.

'So consent is really an issue, but I really think empathy is most important.

'I think it's a constant learning process in a way, not just with 'Night Games', it's that sense of the technical terms or you might go to a website and it will have technical terms for: 'What is domestic violence?' Or 'What is sexual assault?' And then there's the reality. And the reality is always so much more mixed up and there's light and shadow, and there's pain often on all sides, and there's power and there's no power.'

In closing, she adds: 'Until some of these men start choosing to investigate their behaviour and then turning it around and talking to young men and talking to boys and saying, 'Bloody hell, this is what I did and this is how not to do what I did and not to fall into this trap, this bullshit world where I think I'm king,' that's when I think a boy might actually become a man.'

FOUR

CAPSIZES AND CALM: DAMIAN BROWNE'S EPIC SOLO ROW ACROSS THE ATLANTIC

—

SEAN FARRELL | 25 FEBRUARY

THE DAY HAD already been challenging enough.

Christmas had just passed and Damian Browne's morning began with a bang; his head against the wall of his cabin and 'that familiar warm trickle' of blood he felt so often on a rugby field.

Later a curious, but unpredictable, adolescent whale would come to call, circling his craft to set nerves jangling.

Browne was out in the middle of the Atlantic because he wanted a test. He could have happily waited a while longer for this hurdle to come to meet him.

The foot steering on his boat, Darien, had failed and Browne was standing on deck attempting to find a temporary solution. Half-turned, from the corner of his eye, he saw it coming.

The wind tore at its peak, turning the water white and breaking it high and early. The wave came crashing down and put Browne into a cold, salty spin cycle.

He was tethered, he hastens to add, so theoretically couldn't have gone too far from the boat. But instinct told him it was best not to chance it. Amid the chaos of the open ocean, Browne's mind had a clear single task. He clamped his hand onto a handle and was swept under.

'The boat was in the wrong place at the wrong time and I was in the wrong place on the boat at the wrong time,' he tells *The42* now that he's securely back on dry land.

'I had the presence to grab the handles on the cabin hatch, so I just grabbed one of them and around we went.'

Some rugby players go straight into coaching when they retire. Others put their hands up for regular media work or press play on a career path paused since completing college. Damian Browne has refused to let his body off that lightly. He is determined to endure.

The imprints of Browne's rugby career are all over the replies to his absorbing social media posts since beginning an epic solo row across the Atlantic in aid of Médecins Sans Frontières, Madra and The Roots Foundation school in Rwanda.

There, below the line, offering encouragement are former teammates from his time in Connacht and Leinster, Brive and Oyonnax. From John Muldoon to Sean O'Brien, Jordi Murphy to Scott Spedding. They respected the work in his past career, but these feats are making jaws drop.

Since retiring from rugby, Browne has put his body to the most severe of tests, first in the sapping Marathon des Sables in 2016, and now this: 63 days rowing from La Gomera in the Canaries to Antigua. A trip of 4,800 kilometres to place an ocean's worth of scrutiny on his physical ability, of course, but also on the resilience of his mind.

The deep bass of Browne's Galway accent comes down the

line from the quiet lobby of his Antigua hotel. He has had time to catch up on sleep and calories now, but as he looks back, the 37-year-old expresses some regret around both his preparation and approach to the voyage.

In some respects he was not prepared to go to contingency plans. He placed too much faith in his boat and her equipment to stand firm against all that was coming. However, when it came to his own mental state he had the toolbox fully stocked, sharpened and ready to patch up any slight fraying at the seams.

'It's kind of the reason I put myself into these things: I want to be tested mentally as well as physically and see what I'm capable of,' says the former second-row forward.

The answer to that still hasn't necessarily found a limit thanks to constant solidifying maintenance from Browne, working almost as hard to keep his mind on course as his boat.

'I've learned as I've went and evolved a bit. I have some processes that I rely on, like when you get into a negative thought process: resetting.

'I use a mantra or a statement that cuts the negative process. It would be quite a blunt thing you'd say to yourself. Then you'd have some positive statements to say to yourself over and over again to get the mind back into a positive mindset.

'That's the trick really — staying positive in the really mundane times, the hard times.'

Positivity is easier said than done when your body aches, the equipment is giving up and there's nothing but grey waves on the horizon for thousands of kilometres ahead. So Browne made sure to devote time and effort to generating positivity rather than sitting back behind his oars and hoping that it found him.

'In the morning when I wake up I'd just do five minutes of

affirmations, saying stuff like: 'Simply nothing will stop you rowing across the Atlantic,' and, 'You're unbreakable, you're unstoppable, you're indestructible.'

'It might sound a bit corny, but it's incredibly powerful in the medium term. I find if you do it well coming into an event, then it can work very, very well.

'Another one would be, when your mind is a bit out of control, coming back to the things you can control and focus on them. For me, out there, it would have been things like my position in the seat, my effort, my self-talk. So I'd concentrate on those things.'

Browne constantly speaks of being present throughout his task. It can be easy to write off the language of mindfulness as something wishy-washy, replaceable by 'just getting on with it'. But getting on with it is exactly what it allowed Browne to do: next job, control the controllables. Indeed, that approach can prove a life-saver in moments like his capsize, when being present meant focusing on nothing but the strength of his grip to keep hold of the cabin handle while the boat spun through the wave.

'I was able to dial all my mental capacities into my grip. I was like, 'Just squeeze your grip as hard as you can as you go round.'

'Then I was incredibly calm under the water. 'OK, you've thought about this, visualised this, the boat will self-right. You will come around eventually. Just stay as calm as possible and go with it. You don't have to do anything. You will come around.' And eventually it did — I say 'eventually', it might have been only six or seven seconds.'

Eternity when you're underwater against your own volition.

'I never felt any pull. I'm a big believer that you can only control what you can control. I did my bit, and even if I hadn't grabbed the handle I probably would have been okay, but y'know...'

Best not to leave these things to chance.

* * *

'THE FINGERS ARE the real problem.'

After five days back among people, out of the boat and on *terra firma*, Browne has overcome baby giraffe syndrome and regained his land legs. He quickly adapts to a sense that his bedroom is moving each morning and the loss of the tranquility of the open ocean is more than welcome.

Yet his knuckles won't let him forget what they've been through. For 63 days they gripped hard against the handle thrust against them, and pulled, pulled, pulled.

They were firm as he tore through stroke after stroke, wave after wave, hour after hour, day after day until Antigua was just a simple step away.

But now they're solid.

'The joints are basically frozen into place, the knuckle. It's taken a while for them to begin to loosen out and it'll be a while to go yet by the feel of it.

'Even while I was rowing, it was very similar, but you had no choice but to grab the oars and get on with it. After five or 10 minutes the blood flow would loosen them out. But now you don't have that, so grabbing knives, forks and doorknobs, you feel a little bit useless because you can't open anything.'

The advice given to Browne is that normality is just around the corner for his fingers. And thankfully, the same goes for the rest of him. After 63 days of solitary confinement and hard labour, he would be forgiven if his people skills were a little dulled by his experience.

The fact that it was the most familiar figures of his brother Andrew (also a professional rugby player with Connacht), sister Gillian and parents Joe and Mary who were there to offer emotional embraces on his arrival can only have helped the transition back into a social life.

'I remember the first night in particular, I came in around mid-afternoon, I went out for dinner that night with my family and friends.

'It was just a contentment to be around people and have them talking. I could have sat there and not said a word — of course that didn't happen — but I would have been very happy sitting there and have people talk around me.

'The fact that there was pizza and steak there didn't go down badly either after eating out of a bag for 63 days.'

The bags weren't all bad.

Browne bought a little from many sources, adding a little variety to days and weeks that easily blended into one. He needed every ounce of nutrients from his expedition rations, rehydrated to edible state by the addition of boiling water.

Over the course of his epic row, 28 kilogrammes were lost from Browne's 6'5' frame. Heading west after a long taper as a sturdy 130kg lock, Browne arrived on the other side at 102 kg and — bar the full unkempt beard — resembled a fighter in need of a hearty meal after sweating for the week before weigh-in.

The calories expended would have been considerably lower were it not for the technical challenges, however. In the case of the lost oar, he blames himself for skipping necessary stages, seeking a shortcut to keep a protective collar from riding up his oar handle.

After days of loosening the screws to bring the collar back down, one day he had a hammer and so the problem became a nail... until rough seas shook him from the cabin into action and he discovered that the problem was an oar again. As in, he was missing one.

'She's such a monster, the Atlantic. You have to be incredibly on the ball with your checklist of things that have to be done.

'I felt sorry for myself for a few minutes and then berated myself for not being on the ball with that.

'Thankfully, you have to bring two sets of oars, but the problem was, and the reason I was really pissed off at the time, was that I had never used the second set.

'They were a different make than the first set. So the oars I'd trained with and done my first 10 days with were gone. It took a bit of getting used to, heavier, and I just felt this is slowing me down even more.'

You might think that losing an oar would be the biggest problem a rower would face on a trip like this. Far from it: being reduced to using those oars as a means of steering as well as propulsion was the real issue.

'I was foot-steering — there's a rod that goes down from your foot-plate and there's a weld there. Somehow the weld broke and when you're in the middle of the Atlantic, you're a long way from a welder. It's not something you carry.

'It was a huge moment in the crossing, because I was already doing it the rawest way — I had no auto-helm [to control direction], which 95% of the boats had — so I was down to the most crude form of getting across, which is steering with the oars. And when you're steering with the oars you almost need to have one oar in the water at all times, so it doesn't give you much chance to get a lot of speed up.

'It's incredibly draining to steer with the oars. You need a lot of upper body strength, because you're leveraging off one side all the time. You've got tonnes of water on the blade of the oar at all times and you're rowing on the other side. So you need good core stability and strong arms, especially in heavy seas and big conditions.

'At night you'd be absolutely sapped mentally and physically from the day.'

As a result, sleeping sound was never much of an issue. But without the direction of the auto-helm, it was tough to convince the boat to remain facing west through the night.

'When you wake up during the night, you look at what speed you're doing or what direction you're going. Sometimes you'd leave the boat on a certain bearing, 270° or whatever and you wake up at 220° and you're kind of going, 'Will I just pop on the oars and get it back to 270° or let her go in that direction?' I was at the mercy of the winds, but invariably they'd keep you going west.'

Ordinarily, Browne would get about six hours of sleep in a night. A bit of charge in the battery and he was up long before dawn to get moving again. He remained on Spanish time for a sense of consistency, though moving towards the Americas meant the shape of the day became quite disconnected from his clock.

So the routine would look something like this: 6am or 7am, wake up, untie everything he had locked down the night before and row until sunrise and breakfast.

Lunch, an hour's rest and (if there was no maintenance required) possibly a power nap would follow another two-hour stint on the oars. Then a further two hours took him to the hottest part of the day, time to duck back into the cabin to avoid the harshest sunlight.

Then it was back to work until sunset. If the night was well moonlit and clear, he wouldn't even stop there.

'Just try to maximise the daylight, because when you steer with the oars, you need to see where the blade is in the water and you need to see what's coming at you so you can read the waves. When there's no moonlight, it's really really hard.

'You can get the oars slammed into your quads or one in the ribs and it's really, really sore and you're not really going very far. So when conditions weren't so bad and you could row at night, I'd take an hour off and be back rowing from 10pm until 2am.'

That's when all was going to plan. The closer he got to the finish line, the more enticing, and necessary, a bit of overtime became.

'My routine kind of evolved into 12 hours rowing a day. The most I did was 19 — I was trying to fight north after being pushed south 60-odd miles by the wind.

'I was very conscious that I was only 500 or 600 miles from Antigua, getting a lot of calls from the duty officers saying I had to get north.

'I did 19 hours. And the following day I did 13 before I crashed. I was exhausted.'

It's been a hectic year and a half for Browne. Aside from the treacherous 63 days of the Talisker Atlantic Challenge, there was a host of ancillary work that was required behind it.

His strained muscles and blister-coated hands tell the tale of the row, but the fundraising efforts took a toll too. The rest of the Browne family has jetted back to Galway, but Damian will continue his hard-earned recuperation in the Caribbean for a few more weeks.

'Although it sounds a bit strange, I need some space and time,' he says, not realising how much sense he's making. The first bit of decluttering he did after lasting the distance was to bid a business-like goodbye to the craft that carried him.

'I kissed goodbye to it on Sunday, happily,' Browne says, hinting that the kiss was more Michael on Fredo Corleone than a genuinely tender farewell.

'It was kind of a gentle shove away from the dock. They asked me if I wanted to row it out 200 metres; I said, 'No…''

'It was quite a strained relationship. It got me across the Atlantic safe and sound and I'm very, very thankful for that, but we had our issues.'

Perhaps the issues with Darien made her a helpful lightning rod through which Browne could channel his frustration. In any case, they brought about the impressive flexes from his mental strength and left him with a life lesson, writ large, underlined and in bold.

Yet he kept going, hard against the elements, telling himself: 'Keep trying to get up there, because that's the fastest way of getting across.'

'The one thing I came back to time and again was just to keep going, never give up. There were times the little devil on my left shoulder would say, 'Just crawl in there. What's the difference between 51 more days or 52? Or 63 days and 64. Just rest up.' Just to keep going, keep grinding even when times are at their lowest and never give up. That was the one thing I kept coming back to time and again: keep churning away whatever the circumstances.

'To do the hard thing and not just feel sorry for yourself, to keep churning away and trying to get into that position, going forward, even if it's only inching forward. As long as you're going forward and keeping it positive, you'll get where you want to go in the end.

'I kept saying that to myself. Fight from beginning to end. It was never one I was going to win, but I might survive.

'I ended up surviving.'

Having proved himself through such hellish conditions, the achievement feels sweet to Browne as he knocks back cool beer by a tame swimming pool. For most, a few lengths of that might be enough of a challenge to consider for the foreseeable future. Yet the longer you listen to Browne speak about regrets and what he learned from the trip, the stronger the impression that a follow-up is already on the cards.

He is an endurance athlete now, or an adventurer. Whatever profession he might choose for himself, scores of others will call him an inspiration.

'I wouldn't say no to another ocean row. I wouldn't do the same route, because I've done it, and I wouldn't do it solo. I'd like to do it in a team, share the experience with some people. Definitely not ruling it out — I've thought about what I could do or what route I could do.

'It won't be any time soon though. I'm not that sick.'

FIVE

THE LOST GENIUS OF IRISH FOOTBALL: REMEMBERING LIAM WHELAN, DUBLIN'S BUSBY BABE

—

RYAN BAILEY | 5 FEBRUARY

DETACHED FROM THE museum and tourist footfall, the St Paul's section of Glasnevin Cemetery — tucked away to the left of the Finglas Road — can be a lonely place on mornings like this. A glacial wind intermittently swirls from the Phoenix Park direction, briefly subsiding before another harsh gust cuts across moments of peaceful reflection.

There are two other people in sight. An elderly woman, wrapped from the elements in a headscarf, and, further in the distance, a cemetery worker busily clearing leaves.

It's easy to get lost in your thoughts.

A few plots — nine, to be exact — up on the right-hand side from the main entrance, one headstone stands out, not only for its size but for its white granite finish, embellished with a statue of Our Lady of Lourdes on top.

Placed on the grave are red and white flowers with a Manchester United club scarf wrapped around a vase inscribed with the family name. It's immaculately maintained and beautifully poignant.

In Loving Memory of My Dear Son Liam Whelan,
Of 28, St Attracta Road, Cabra,
Manchester United AFC.
Who died in the Munich Air Disaster,
6th February 1958,
Aged 22 years.

Those words resonate like never before.

Maybe it's an age thing, maybe it's just the week that's in it. Either way, there is a deep, profound connection.

There is an understanding, and greater appreciation, of what happened, who he was and how the devastating events of 6 February 1958 had such a reverberating effect through so many lives, so close to home.

* * *

LAST SATURDAY, A large crowd gathered under the Munich Clock, in the south-east corner of Old Trafford, as the 23 victims of the Munich Air Disaster were remembered through prayers, readings and a moving rendition of 'The Flowers of Manchester'.

The East Stand's all-glass facade, overlooking the main stadium forecourt, has three large banners running vertically, the centrepiece being a printed replica of the Munich Clock which sits over the statue of Sir Matt Busby. On either side, a list of names.

Geoff Bent
Roger Byrne
Eddie Colman
Duncan Edwards
Mark Jones
David Pegg
Tommy Taylor
Liam 'Billy' Whelan.
The Busby Babes.
The English League Champions.
The Flowers of Manchester.

For so many people, for so many reasons, this isn't an ordinary match day.

The visit of Huddersfield Town to Old Trafford may outwardly be a peripheral fixture in the context of Manchester United's season, but there is more to this day than football. And particularly this year, the 60th year.

As part of the commemorations, the current Manchester United players wear black armbands and kick off is preceded by a minute's silence, during which Old Trafford falls deathly silent. It carries significance, and undiluted emotion.

Sitting in the Directors' Box are the families of the victims alongside one of only two remaining survivors, Sir Bobby Charlton, and they will return again later today for a service at Old Trafford, which on days like this truly is a special place, and not just the commercialised version it is often portrayed to be.

Similarly, the same can be said about Manchester United as a club.

74,742 were inside Old Trafford to watch Jose Mourinho's side win 2-0 and, for the majority, that's what mattered. It's what they came to see. But perhaps they left — some heading back to far-flung places — with a better education and understanding of what makes the club they've come to worship the way it is.

And why whatever happens on the field, there is a timeless aura of indomitability and a sense of identity forged by the collective suffering through the years. And why there is a Munich Clock and Tunnel forever remembering the men lost on that dark day.

And why those who died in Munich became an eternal flame in Manchester United's history and thus a guiding light for everything the club has gone on to become and achieve.

* * *

IT'S HARD TO imagine how the crowds managed to all congregate on this side of the cemetery as they did for the funeral. One of the gravediggers told the family he had not seen as many people in Glasnevin since the burial of Michael Collins.

The pictures, although a little grainy, are staggering. You can see rows and rows of people, men and women, young and old, as the heartbreak felt in Manchester extended to an unprecedented outpouring of grief on the streets of Dublin. The city came to a standstill.

The funeral cortege from Dublin Airport to Christ the King Church in Cabra was flanked by thousands upon thousands, as Liam Whelan arrived home on 10 February 1958, four days after he lost his life when British European Airways flight 609 failed to take off on its third attempt at Munich-Riem Airport. He was just 22. He was Dublin's Busby Babe.

Eight Manchester United players suffered fatal injuries on that inexplicably tragic day, and 15 other passengers —

including three members of club staff and eight members of the travelling press — were killed. Matt Busby's young team were on their way back from a European Cup tie in Belgrade. They were the future of the club, they represented everything about the club. And then Munich. Such shock, such loss.

'Words cannot describe the devastating effect that this disaster had on the football club and the lives of those affected,' Sir Bobby Charlton wrote in a recent letter to Manchester United's current players. 'This great football club, which you are part of, has risen from its darkest hour in a way like no other.'

* * *

TWO HOURS HAVE passed and we've barely scratched the surface. Lost in a myriad of stories, both happy and sad, Christy and John Whelan replay moments in time over in their mind.

They reminisce with pride and great affection and remember how their brother scored twice for Manchester United against Shamrock Rovers at Dalymount Park, how he was man of the match in an FA Cup final in front of 100,000 at Wembley, and how his record of scoring in eight successive top-flight games was only broken by Ruud van Nistelrooy 45 years later.

'They were all happy days,' Christy smiles.

Despite his remarkable goalscoring record — better than one every other game from the inside-forward position — and role in back-to-back league winning sides under Busby, Liam Whelan's career was only really blossoming when it was so cruelly cut short.

He was the quiet and reserved member of the Busby Babes, but let his performances and goals do the talking, scoring 52 goals in 96 Manchester United appearances.

'He would fetch a fortune today,' says his older brother, who was Liam's biggest supporter, travelling near and far to watch him playing for Home Farm and then with Manchester United.

Leggy and rake-thin, Whelan was best recognised for his deadly finishing but it was his ball control, vision, mesmerising dribbling ability and capacity to glide past defenders which made him stand out. He could pass, dribble, shoot and finish. He had a wand of a right foot. He had it all.

In a young side nurtured and moulded by Busby and his assistant Jimmy Murphy, containing the likes of Charlton and Duncan Edwards, Whelan was the schemer, the playmaker. He made things tick.

'One of the games we went over to was Blackpool at Old Trafford and the great Stanley Matthews was playing,' Christy recalls. 'We were in the near stand at the time and the ball was over the far side and Matthews had it.

'He was rolling the ball and went by somebody, I forget who it was, but who appeared, only Liam. And he took the ball off him and stood in front of Matthews and just kept rolling the ball back and forward down by the corner flag and nutmegged him.

'And the crowd stood up in the stand: 'Go on, Billy! Show them what ball-playing is all about.'

'I never forgot that.'

* * *

LATER ON TUESDAY, Home Farm FC will host an event to mark the 60th anniversary of Liam Whelan's passing, during which a wreath will be laid to commemorate, and celebrate, the life and career of the club's most famous export. They're proud of him around these parts, and he was proud to be from Cabra.

His connection with home remained strong during his four years in Manchester, and Whelan, a devout Catholic who suffered from terrible homesickness, would jump on the B&I Ferry back to Dublin as often as he could.

'We used to go down and meet him at the North Wall,' John remembers. 'The boat took 14 hours from Liverpool and there were times he used to come home and never say a word and just walk in the door.

'My mother's favourite saying then was, 'When are you going back?' because she wanted to know how long he'd be with us.'

Born to Elizabeth and John Whelan of St Attracta Road on 1 April 1935, Liam was one of seven children — Bridie, Alice, Christy, Liam, Rita, Maura and John — but the family tragically lost their father when Liam was just eight, although his love of soccer had already been handed down to the eldest son Christy, who had been going to nearby Dalymount Park since the age of five.

Christy himself was a fine player in the League of Ireland, but he soon gave up his own career to follow his younger brother, who was fast becoming the star after first kicking a ball in a playground not far from the family home.

'Liam played in the playground very regularly and there was a team called Red Rockets,' Christy explains. 'They used to go around playing in Dublin city and were unbeaten for two years.

'From that, someone suggested he go to join Home Farm and he started playing there at 13. It was a long way away for us at the time with no cars so he used to cycle up to the club. He went from Under-14 right up, and played a year above himself as well as his own team.

'He got a schoolboy cap for Ireland then and they played England at Goodison Park and won that game 8-4. Liam didn't score but he was the best player on the pitch that day.'

On the back of that performance, several of the Irish team were invited for trials at Manchester United and a couple of them — Paddy Kennedy and Noel McFarlane — were offered contracts at Old Trafford. But there was no interest in Liam, and despite standing out in Home Farm colours, that continued for another couple of years.

'I didn't miss one game he played for Home Farm and I used to come home wondering why there wasn't anybody [scouts] coming to see him play,' Christy says, shaking his head, still to this day bemused by it.

'I used to be saying this to my mother all the time: 'I don't know what's going wrong here, people in this country don't see it but Liam is the best player I've seen in this country."

* * *

THERE WERE FIVE tables, each of 10 people, all from completely different backgrounds and walks of life, but all united by Munich. Some knew each other from these events down through the years, others had been passed the baton to carry on the legacy of their loved one.

There were brothers, sisters, sons, daughters, nieces, nephews, cousins, grandchildren, great nieces, great nephews and great-grandchildren, but there was no generation gap. Just an afternoon of mournful reflection and a celebration of everything the Busby Babes stood for through the exchange of stories. It was special.

Hearing how Northern Ireland's Jackie Blanchflower

suffered injuries so severe that he would never play again and how Harry Gregg, who was sitting beside Liam on ill-fated flight 609 but escaped the burning wreckage to save some of his team-mates, including Charlton, could not bring himself to attend this anniversary event because a return to Old Trafford carried too much emotion. He was represented by his son-in-law.

To this day, each family is affected in different ways, but above everything, there is a great sense of pride. There were more smiles and laughs than tears, and words cannot describe the honour felt when Old Trafford rose to show its appreciation for the Munich families as they were welcomed into the Director's Box.

The affection for the beloved Busby Babes has remained as strong as ever over the last six decades, and on days like this, members of that special team, one which ultimately shaped the future of Manchester United, are in the hearts and minds of supporters, both from Manchester and beyond.

As many as 2,000 supporters have travelled to Munich for a commemoration service while a similar event will take place in Belgrade, where, by pure coincidence, Manchester United's Under-19 team are preparing for a Uefa Youth Cup tie. The old Stadion JNA, just like Old Trafford and Home Farm FC, will fall silent at 3.04pm, the exact time a great football team met destruction.

* * *

I MAY 1953.
'I had been up in Home Farm that evening,' Christy recalls. 'They were playing Merrion Rovers and Billy Behan [Manchester

United scout] had Bert Whalley [coach] with him and they came over to see Vinny Ryan. He was a great schoolboy at that time as well and went to Glasgow Celtic afterwards, but they had come to sign him for United.

'Liam played well that day. He was brilliant. Just before half-time, Bert Whalley turns to Billy Behan and says, 'I don't want Ryan, get Whelan and get him as soon as you can.'"

Through the vision of Matt Busby, who held the view that the only way to lay long-lasting foundations for success was through youth, Manchester United placed huge emphasis on developing their own talent, and at the same time created a pattern and philosophy which ran right through from their underage teams to the first team; a free-flowing, thrilling and attractive brand of football which revolutionised the English game.

The Busby Babes offered a template for entertaining football that quickly became the central ideology of Manchester United, and at 18 years of age, a supremely talented young Irish inside-forward fit perfectly into that mould.

'We came home and I was in bed that night, it was fairly late, and half asleep,' Christy continues. 'The bedroom door opened and a hand started shaking my shoulder. 'Christy, Christy,' and I turned and looked, it was Liam. 'Can you come downstairs?' he asked.

'I thought there was something wrong. 'There's some man here from Manchester United,' he said, to which I replied; 'It's about bloody time.'

'We had no dressing gowns so it was an overcoat I put on and went downstairs and Billy Behan was standing there in the living room with Tom Smith from Home Farm.

'Billy just said, 'We want Liam to go over to Manchester United. We want him to play for Manchester United.'

'I remember turning to my mother and she said, 'Christy, they want to take him away'... She didn't want it. She wanted it for Liam but the thought of one of us leaving the house didn't sit well with her.

'I said to Billy Behan, 'What is he going over for?' and he said, 'He's going over to play in United's youth team.' I said, 'Is he going over for a trial? Because he's too good for a trial.'

"No, no trials,' Behan said.

"Okay, that's okay with me,' I said, and that was that. Billy made all the arrangements for a flight over and he went straight away. Off he went at 18.

'I cried that night.'

* * *

THERE WAS A strong Irish connection at Manchester United at the time. Noel McFarlane, Tommy Hamilton, Jackie Mooney, Joe Carolan, Jackie Hennessy and a young Johnny Giles were all also on the books at Old Trafford during the 1950s, becoming great friends.

Some came and went without ever really making their mark on the first team, but Whelan made an instant impact, starring in the FA Youth Cup final win over Wolves just three days after he signed for the club.

With local lad John Doherty out injured, Whelan was drafted straight into an extraordinarily gifted team containing Kennedy, McFarlane, Eddie Colman, Duncan Edwards, David Pegg and Albert Scanlon, and they won the first leg 7-1 at Old Trafford, with Manchester United's new recruit scoring the final goal late on before finding the net during a 2-2 second leg draw.

The club would dominate the FA Youth Cup for the first five years of the competition's existence and Busby's policy of investing in youth and building teams of world-class footballers was now in full swing.

Not only did the Scot, who had taken his first steps into management with Manchester United in 1945, foster a seismic transition but he was bold and brave enough to change the guard and introduce a raft of young rookies into the team.

Whelan had to bide his time before getting his opportunity, but Busby knew of the Irishman's talent and potential from the outset, particularly after his performances during a youth tournament in Bern, during which watching scouts from Brazilian club Santos made enquiries about his availability.

'He was brilliant and the Brazilians at times stood up and clapped him, they couldn't believe how good he was,' John remembers. 'The skill he had, he had tremendous skill on the ball. He got man of the match and the Brazilians talked to Matt Busby that day.

'But Busby said: 'He's going nowhere. If they think they can make him the best player in the world, we can do that."

* * *

SITTING IN THE shadow of Old Trafford Cricket Ground, 42 Great Stone Road is a small semi-detached, red-brick house on a quiet street in the suburb of Stretford. It's just a short, straight walk up towards Old Trafford via Sir Matt Busby Way and not far from Manchester city centre.

The greenery is a little overgrown in the front garden and barely recognisable from the last time Christy Whelan was there back in 1954, on one of the many trips over to visit his brother.

'It's completely different to how I imagined it,' he laughs, looking at a photograph he's just taken out of his wallet. 'There you are now.'

Standing in the driveway are Mrs Whelan, Joe Carolan, Johnny Giles, Christy and the housekeeper Ms Gibbs, who watered and fed Liam and Bobby Charlton during the two years they shared the residence together.

During that time, Whelan was learning his trade for Manchester United's reserve team in the harsh environments of the Central League but his class shone through, becoming a prolific goalscorer to quickly turn the head of Busby.

'He really started shining then,' says John.

Five days short of his 20th birthday, the young forward was called upon for Manchester United's First Division game against Preston North End at Deepdale on 26 March 1955.

His first game at senior level ended in a 2-0 victory thanks to goals from Roger Byrne and Scanlon, and the following week Whelan scored the first of his 52 goals in red in a 5-0 demolition of Sheffield United at Old Trafford.

'In his first full season, United won the league by an incredible 11 points but Liam had only played 13 games and you needed to play a third of them to get a medal,' John continues. 'But somehow Matt got Liam a medal and then the following year, he was an ever-present in the team.'

The Babes were taking English football by storm. Liam Whelan was at the heart of it.

Unbeaten in their first dozen league games in 1956-57, Busby's side were cutting teams apart at will and while they had a settled core to the team, such was the strength in depth, and calibre of young player at the club, that season also marked the arrival of a certain Bobby Charlton.

Back-to-back league crowns were secured by a margin of 11 points from Tottenham Hotspur and Preston, with United's high-scoring forwards racking up more than a century of First Division goals during the campaign, with Whelan leading the way on 26.

'Thirty-three goals altogether in that season between FA Cup and European Cup,' Christie states. 'He had a tremendous season, and you have to remember Tommy Taylor and Dennis Viollet were spearheading United's attack that season. It was a staggering achievement.

'That year John went over during Easter for the Burnley game. He wrote to Liam before going over to say he was coming with a group from Home Farm. Anyway, he scored twice that day at Turf Moor and needless to say we were over the moon. Proud as anything.'

* * *

OFF THE FIELD, Liam Whelan was a quiet, shy and humble character. He longed for home but at the same time began to settle into life in Manchester — where he was known as Billy — growing up alongside his team-mates in shared digs, creating a formidable and unbreakable team spirit among a young squad.

Both Whelan and the club were reaching rarefied heights, and after their domestic success, soon became European trailblazers despite pressure from the Football Association to decline the opportunity to play on the continent, like Chelsea had done the previous year.

The FA did not want the midweek European travel to affect domestic fixtures but the single-minded and visionary Busby ignored the traditionalists and in realising the boundless benefits of competing against other league winners, refused to bow to higher powers.

In the 1957-58 European Cup, Manchester United were drawn against Shamrock Rovers in the preliminary round, with the first leg of the tie taking place at Dalymount Park. It was the first time a League of Ireland club had qualified for the competition and the game was all the talk around Dublin at the time.

'That was some night,' Christy says, brimming with pride.

Working in the Corporation at the time, one of his colleagues had organised a sweepstake for the first goalscorer and, rather inevitably, Christy drew his brother, who was lining out in the red of United.

'Liam scored twice, but unfortunately it was the wrong two goals he scored,' he laughs.

'The sweep was half a dollar a man, that was two shillings and a sixpence. That was a good bit of money.

'When Liam was leaving the house that evening to go to Dalymount I said, 'Hey Mister, I have you in the sweep in work.' 'Good,' he said and off he went.

'There wasn't too long gone in the match and the ball came over and unusually for him he missed a wide-open goal. He missed it and cost me the money! But he scored the second and the third goal and United won 6-0. He had a brilliant game.'

With family members dotted around various parts of Dalymount Park, that was a particularly memorable night for the Whelans.

'My mother was in the stand and there were tears,' Christy continues.

'The one thing that Liam's two uncles used to say was 'if only Johnny was alive'. That was my father. He was fanatical about soccer and I remember Stephen was over in the house after that match.

'I was sitting beside him and he turned to me. 'You know something, Christy? The saddest part about it all is that he didn't live to get to see him, Liam. He would have loved it.' And he was right. It was a great shame.'

* * *

THERE ISN'T MUCH footage of Liam Whelan in action available, but the clips that are online provide a perfect snapshot of the type of player he was. See his stunning, virtuoso goal in the European Cup quarter-final against Athletic Bilbao as the prime example.

With United trailing 5-2 in the snow and mud, Busby's side were heading towards elimination when, with five minutes of the first leg remaining, Whelan produced a remarkable moment of individual brilliance to spark an incredible comeback.

Collecting the ball in the middle of the field, he skips past three would-be tacklers before cutting back inside onto his powerful right foot to rifle home into the top-corner from the edge of the area.

'People always remember Liam for his goals, but we remember him for his ability. He was just a brilliant footballer in a brilliant team,' continues John.

United went on to win the second leg 3-0 and advance to the semi-finals, where their first European odyssey ended at the hands of Real Madrid. That was five months before Munich. Disaster lurked around the corner.

* * *

'IT SHOULDN'T HAVE happened,' Christy says, bowing his head. 'It shouldn't have happened. It wouldn't happen nowadays.'

The Busby Babes were near-certainties to complete a hat-trick of league titles in the 1957-58 season, and as more talented young players came through the system and the established stars reached their prime, the potential of the team knew no bounds.

There also seemed every chance that an elusive, and much sought-after, League and Cup double — having lost the 1957 FA Cup final to Aston Villa — would become a reality at last and having reached the last four of the European Cup at the first attempt, there was no reason why they couldn't go two steps further second time around.

After an early slump in form, including three defeats in four games, Busby made a couple of bold changes to his side, as he dropped Ray Wood, Johnny Berry, David Pegg and Whelan, with his close friend Charlton occupying the inside-forward position.

Busby's decision was instantly vindicated as United's form and results turned a corner and they embarked on a run of nine games unbeaten but because of the tragic events to come, Whelan's last game for the club was in a 1-0 defeat to Chelsea in December 1957.

Having been beset by a bout of the flu, while also hearing news from back home of his mother's bad health, he remained out of the team at the expense of Charlton by the time United reached the quarter-finals of the European Cup.

After safely advancing past Shamrock Rovers in that famous tie, they made light work of Dukla Prague to set up a last eight date with Red Star Belgrade in January 1958.

Busby's side were far from their clinical best in the first leg but managed to emerge with a 2-1 victory before travelling to

Belgrade for the second leg on 5 February 1958. They drew 3-3 but advanced to a second successive European semi-final 5-4 on aggregate.

The great tragedy is that Whelan had sought permission from Busby to return home to Dublin for a few days, but the United manager wanted the whole squad to travel to Serbia in a show of unity.

'It was only a matter of time before Liam got back in the team but he wanted to come home,' John explains. 'You could see where Matt was coming from because if anyone got injured, there was no sense in Liam being in Dublin.

'But he wanted to come home to make arrangements for his wedding. That's what I thought anyway. He was engaged to Ruby and they were due to get married the following summer but that was it, he went on the trip. God knows his own ways.'

* * *

'THE TRAGIC NEWS *of Liam Whelan's death reached his family home at St Attracta Road, Cabra, late last night, after hours of agonised waiting. From the time the first reports of the disaster reached Dublin, crowds gathered at the Whelan home and phone calls for news of Liam were put through to Manchester at regular intervals on a phone in a neighbour's house. Schoolboy friends waited silently, hoping against hope for the word that he survived.'* — THE IRISH PRESS, *7 February* 1958.

After celebrating their victory at the post-match banquet the night before, Manchester United's players boarded the twin-engined British European Airways plane, flight 609, for their journey back to Manchester via Munich to refuel.

Upon arrival at a snow-covered and sub-zero Munich-Riem Airport, the squad got off the plane to spend some time in the terminal building before embarking on the second leg of their trip home. Shortly after 2pm local time, the 44 passengers were back on the aircraft and the first of three aborted take-off attempts was made.

As the pilot attempted to get the aircraft, known as the Lord Burleigh, off the ground, the engine made a strange noise and captain James Thain and his co-pilot Kenneth Rayment slammed on the brakes, stopping just 400 yards from the end of the runway.

A couple of minutes later, a second attempt was abandoned in near identical circumstances, before the aircraft was taxied back to the terminal to be examined by engineers on the ground. At that stage, everyone on board returned to the relative warmth of the lounge.

By 3.02pm, a decision had been made. The pilot informed the control tower that they would try again, for a third time. The engineers were satisfied that the noise didn't pose a safety threat and Thain was content that the wings hadn't iced over.

Passengers who survived have since described the mood as apprehensive, but there wasn't a great deal of panic, although the previous boisterous mood as the players played cards had silenced considerably. Some, including Duncan Edwards, Tommy Taylor and Mark Jones, had decided to move to the back of the aircraft in the hope it was safer.

'It was an awful decision,' John says. 'There were actually photographs of some of the players sweeping snow off the wings. They were under pressure to get home. They had a league fixture to fulfil on the Saturday.'

The aircraft failed to gather enough speed on the icy surface, overshooting the runway and smashing through the perimeter fence and into a nearby house. As the plane hurtled along the slushy runway and towards destruction, Liam uttered the chilling words: 'If this is the end, then I am ready for it.'

The cockpit hit a tree and part of the fuselage slammed into an airport fuel hut, which instantly exploded. The wing and part of the back were torn off. Some were killed instantly, others lay among the debris unconscious and beyond help. Utter destruction and devastation.

Back home in Dublin, the Whelan family learned of the shattering news hours after it had first broken.

'I was sitting in a chair like this in front of the fire at the time and the next thing I heard the gate,' Christy recalls.

'My mother and Alice were out the back ironing and I saw it was Charlie Jackson, who used to look after Liam's team in Home Farm. He was a good friend of the family.

'I shouted out, 'Here's Charlie,' and my mother came into the front room and pointed at the clock and said, 'They're home Charlie, they're home.'

"I'm afraid not, Mrs Whelan,' he said.

"What's wrong, Charlie? They're home, Charlie.'

"Have you not heard?' he said. 'I've come up to offer my condolences and to be with you when we're waiting. The plane has crashed.'

'The whole of Dublin knew and we didn't,' Christy continues, looking to the sky. 'We were all in here and we hadn't heard.'

As news filtered through and the whole picture emerged, the scale of the tragedy became agonisingly clear.

'We would get the bulletins and they were going through all the names: Geoff Bent — dead. Eddie Colman — dead. Tommy Taylor — dead. But there was no mention of Liam.

The house was full of people but we all knew.

'We eventually got a phone call and I went in and it was Jimmy Murphy...

"Christy, we've bad news,' he said. 'Liam didn't survive. From what's left here at Old Trafford, we send our sympathies. We'll be in touch and will help you through this.'

'My mother insisted on leaving the radio on in case news came through that he had survived. She didn't want to believe it. She took it badly and late that night, she came into me and said: 'Christy, if he was dead, wouldn't the police have come to us?'

He pauses, before adding: 'And I had to tell her... I had to tell her that the police had come and given official notice of Liam's death.'

* * *

LIAM WHELAN'S PRODIGIOUS talent may have been extinguished, but his legacy and legend has grown over the years since his death. His record for Manchester United speaks for itself and it's widely acknowledged that he was not just cut down in his prime, but before he had even reached it.

Described as the lost talent of Irish football, Whelan was nudging greatness when tragedy intruded, and it was perhaps his unassuming disposition, and reluctance to appear in the media, that cost him the affection in which some of his team-mates were held.

But from anyone who knew him, played with him or watched him play, there was nothing but adulation and admiration for one of the finest players of his generation who would have undoubtedly gone on to even greater things.

He earned four international caps for the Boys in Green

during Ireland's qualifying campaign for the 1958 World Cup, but was cruelly denied the opportunity to truly fulfil his potential both for club and country.

Under the tutelage of Busby and Murphy, and playing alongside such gifted players at Old Trafford, the horizon for Whelan appeared boundless. Without question, he was one of the greatest footballers Ireland has ever produced.

Even more heartbreaking was the fact he was due to be joined in Manchester by his soon-to-be wife Ruby and the pair planned on settling down together in England, which would certainly have eased his homesickness and helped his performances on the pitch. Alas, it wasn't to be.

'He had a great career for the time he was there but if he hadn't have been homesick he would have been even better,' Christy laments.

Whelan's death left a hole as big as any at Old Trafford, where he was revered but it was back home in Cabra where he was beloved both personally and professionally by those who knew him, grew up with him and followed him.

'Liam loved to stay involved with the community,' Christy continues. 'There was a five-a-side tournament in Dalymount Park and Liam brought a team over from England. He was home in the house anyway and a few kids, maybe six- to eight-year-olds, knocked on the door and asked, 'Is Liam coming out?'

'He had just played in the FA Cup final at Wembley but Liam wouldn't say no to anybody. He gave them money to go to the shop up by the bridge [now named after him] to buy a ball and when they got back, he was out playing on the road with them.

'He was so popular. He never gave anyone any reason to say 'that fella is a bloody snob'. When he was home, he'd stop and chat to everyone. He was so loved and we saw that at the funeral. It was a sad occasion.'

In just four years at Manchester United, he left a lasting legacy and achieved immortality through his gifted performances in red and the part he had to play in the evolution and success of the Busby Babes.

His team-mates were all universal in praise. 'As a youngster, I always wanted to be the best player in the world but as long as Liam Whelan was around I doubted if I could,' Bobby Charlton wrote in his book, providing another indication of just how highly he was rated.

'God knows how good he would have been,' John remarks, desperate to know the answer. But at the end of the day, football and goals and caps is all a trivial matter in the greater context of the tragedy to befall Matt Busby's thrilling, pioneering young team.

Lives, futures and families were shattered on that indelible day, today 60 years ago.

'It's hard to believe it's that long ago,' Christy adds. 'But one thing is for sure: Liam is never forgotten. He's never forgotten and never will be.

'My mother had a very good way of looking at it and she always said 'God wanted Liam' and that helped us a lot. It got us through those days and weeks and months and years. It gets us through even now all these years after. God wanted Liam and that's how we saw it.

'We are all so proud of him and the memories have always been there. He was so skilful and they [the press] used to say he was slow, but he could get there! He could take them all on and beat them. He was terrific, he was a terrific boy.

'Liam will never be forgotten and even long after we're gone, his memory will be kept going by the rest of the family.'

'I TOOK ALL THE MONEY OUT OF THE HOUSE, ALL OUR WAGES, AND GAMBLED IT ALL IN 28 MINUTES'

—

SINÉAD FARRELL | 9 DECEMBER

WILLY O'CONNOR was just 10 years of age when he placed his first bet.

It was 1988 and he was on a football trip to Liverpool with a local club, carrying the £10 that his mother gave him for the journey.

A slot machine captured his young imagination on the way over and he decided to take a chance.

He changed the money into coins, and made his way over to the machine with his tracksuit bottoms sliding down slightly with the weight of the money in his pockets.

He squandered £9 in consecutive bets and had just £1 left.

And with his last remaining coin, he pushed the button one final time to see a clean sweep of sevens illuminate the screen in front of him.

He'd hit the mother lode — £25 sterling. For a child in the late '80s it felt more like £25,000 and it made him an instant hit with his teammates when he paid for them all to go to the cinema.

'The gambler wants to be a big shot,' he tells *The42* in a Dublin café.

* * *

THE CHASE AND THE CONSEQUENCES

For the rest of his gambling life, right up until his last bet in 2010, O'Connor hunted for that feeling of euphoria again and again.

'There's a bigger high from gambling than there is from cocaine,' he says.

'The feeling you get, I was chasing that all the time. They say you're chasing the dragon. The more money I lost, the more money I chased to win back.

'You couldn't leave. No matter what, you wanted to double it, treble it and quadruple it. They call that the dream world of the compulsive gambler. You want to have big houses and big yachts, you think you're going to win a couple of million.'

He thought he was just a lucky 10-year-old who stumbled upon the jackpot. But what seemed like a meaningless moment of good fortune for the Clontarf GAA man ultimately led him down a path of self-destruction.

It ruined his marriage and saw him kicked out of the family home. He stole money from his mother and his ex-wife. It drove him to a suicide attempt.

He robbed purses, maxed out credit cards and even dipped into the money pot that was needed for mortgage repayments.

He had different pockets in his trousers for the various people that he owed money to.

On the first night of their honeymoon in Las Vegas,

O'Connor waited for his wife to fall asleep before slipping off to the casino with a fistful of dollars.

He often brought his young children to betting shops and left them sitting in the car with the window down. Other times, he had them in the bookies writing on dockets.

He knew where this was all headed. He knew this would destroy his life. But a force much darker and deeper than love had taken hold of him.

Gambling addiction 'is rife in the GAA', according to O'Connor, and several prominent figures from within the sport have spoken out about their struggles.

All-Ireland winner Oisín McConville, Galway hurler Davy Glennon and recently retired Offaly footballer Niall McNamee have all played their part in raising awareness about the scourge, while several others continue to suffer in silence.

For O'Connor, he's enjoying his second chance at 39. He's currently the kitman with the All-Ireland winning Dublin Ladies. He's also a referee and is still playing some sport himself.

Along with his kitman duties, he works alongside team analyst Seaghan Kearney for the Dublin Ladies, where his numerical skills from his gambling days come in handy for when he's compiling his notes for the stats and analysis.

His daughter Caoimhe is also playing with the Dublin minors.

Life is good for him now, but it has taken a lot of effort on his part to rehabilitate himself.

O'Connor didn't gamble much after winning his £25 jackpot at 10 years of age. The problem lay dormant within him throughout much of his teenage years and while he was in the army.

But just like other addictions, it manifested itself gradually.

Saturday morning bets soon became a Saturday afternoon activity, before spiraling into a 24-hour obsession.

He gravitated to games where results were instant, and he found a passion in the dogs and the roulette machines. By the time online gambling had sunk its claws into him, he was getting his thrills from virtual races.

'The pattern of the way I bet comes from that day when I was 10 because I won the money after one press of a button in less than two seconds.

'The gambling I did all my life after that was all quick.

'I wouldn't back golf because it took four days. I didn't like backing matches because it took 90 minutes. I wanted it on the spot. The dogs was 27 seconds around the track so I used to love the dogs on a Saturday morning.

'By the time I got to do the football all my money was gone on the dogs. I'd lose everything before I even did the football bet. I got into the dogs and I loved them.'

* * *

THE ART OF DECEPTION

O'Connor held down various jobs to fund his gambling. Along with borrowing money from others, he delivered pizzas and started working as a taxi driver after buying a house in 2005.

The house bills were eating into the money he needed for betting, and the taxi fares gave him another outlet to get cash in hand quickly.

His sole focus was on his gambling. During his splurges, he couldn't even spare some money to buy food. Every penny he had was needed for betting.

O'Connor found ways of convincing himself he didn't have a problem and all those who voiced their concerns were to be avoided.

'*What do they know?*
'*They don't know me.*
'*You're grand.*'

On one occasion, he took a break for three months after losing €1,300 in one hour, which forced him to ask his best friend for a loan to pay the mortgage.

But even the fright he got from that experience couldn't keep him away for long. Nothing could stop him from descending further into addiction.

He piled lie upon lie, misery upon misery, and poured it all into a betting docket with dreams of landing a big win that would fix everything.

'Gambling came before everything, ahead of the kids, ahead of everything,' says O'Connor.

'But it never stopped me because gambling was much more powerful than I was and I couldn't stop it.

'You keep going and keep going and you don't leave with the money. The odd time I left was when it was closed but I could never leave.

'No matter what I won, I wanted to go again and go again. I often left with not a penny in my pocket after being up thousands.

'I often went out to the car looking for coins to go back in and win the thousands I was after leaving in there. That's what you do.'

Unlike alcoholism or drug abuse where the evidence is often written all over the victim's face, gambling is largely a silent affliction.

And O'Connor was skilled at keeping it a secret. He could lose thousands in one sitting and still conceal the damage from those around him.

Even when the bills were naturally piling up, he would cover his tracks by calling up the postman to intercept the letters before his wife saw them.

He was always inventing ways to avoid getting caught.

'I always had a story ready. One night I was in the casino and I took €400 out of the account.

'My wife saw it online and asked me about it and I said I was out and that such and such was stuck so I lent him €100 and that he'd give it back.

'I went to my mother's the next day to borrow money. I went to the bookies and won €2,000 and then went back to my wife with the money and said, 'There's that money, he paid me back.'

'She could only believe it. A compulsive gambler is a compulsive liar at the same time because you're very good at it and you always have the story ready.

'People are so busy in their own lives that it's easy for a compulsive gambler to do it because you're cute, you're sharp, and you're always a step ahead. And no-one has a clue.'

He continues: 'My mother caught me a few times over in Kilbarrack outside a bookies with the kids in the car. She'd look out and I'd run out and say I was just collecting a few pounds.

'I didn't go there the next day because she'd catch me so I'd go over to Edenmore and leave the kids sweating in the car and I'd be in the bookies for an hour or two. I'd leave the window down a small bit and they'd be in there crying.'

* * *

CAN'T BEAT THE BOOKIES

There's a line in Oisín McConville's autobiography 'The Gambler' in which he describes gambling as a game where the opposition always wins.

O'Connor had some big wins in his time, but the wins are never the end point. It never stops. Even when he was winning, he was losing.

'That's Paddy Power's money,' was his mantra for justifying his need to keep gambling.

His schemes were often simple, but he could never pull them off.

During one particular moment of desperation, he decided to sell his taxi plate in order to pay some money he owed to his mother and cover other payments. He got over €6,000 for the plate, and the plan was to buy it back with his winnings, while also putting some aside for his mother.

He doubled his money twice that day and saw his earnings rise and fall dramatically. €12,000 soon dropped to €10,000, then €2,000, and later back up to €8,000. He had no control of the situation and his plan quickly unravelled.

'I was high as a kite and my emotions were the same as the money. Up and down like a gambler.

'I couldn't leave and at about 10 past four, the whole lot was gone. I went back to the house like a zombie and then you have to put the brave face on when you get to the house. Your stomach is actually in knots and nearly getting sick.

'[My wife] opens the door and she had to put something in the boot. The taxi plate would either be in the boot or on the roof so she looked in the boot and [there was] no taxi plate.

'She asked where it was and I just said I rented it out, that I was doing too many hours. I told her I'd get €50 a week to put towards the shopping.

'The taxi plate was long sold. I never even told her that. She only found that out a couple of years ago.'

* * *

ROCK BOTTOM

By the time O'Connor placed his last bet on 30 April 2010, he was well aware that his addiction was out of control.

He was neglecting his responsibilities to his children, was snapping at those around him and his humour completely depended on whether or not he had money for gambling.

He was working in Dublin Airport on the day he splurged all of his family's money in under half an hour.

'I took all the money out of the house, all our wages, all my wife's wages and gambled it all in 28 minutes. That's when I had to go home and tell them I was a gambler,' he recalls.

Later that day, he ran into his boss and admitted to his problem. His boss could relate to his pain; O'Connor quit his job and agreed to go home and have the conversation he had avoided for so long.

But on the way, he decided to take another course of action.

'I got on my bike that day and cycled home. On the way home I said, 'They'd be better off if I wasn't fucking around."

He did make it home and told his wife the truth. 'I don't think she'll ever forget that day.

'She didn't know what to say. She was heartbroken. I was gone out of the house after that and I've been gone out of it ever since. She asked me to leave and when I think back, she was right because I'd never have stopped if she didn't put me out.'

O'Connor attended his first Gamblers Anonymous (GA) meeting after that in Gardiner Street in Dublin, where he met three people he had already come across in the bookies.

It was painful to acknowledge the problem in front of strangers but his path to recovery had begun.

* * *

RECOVERY

It took a long time for O'Connor to rebuild his life. He wasn't allowed to have a bank card for two years, and could only be trusted with €1 when attending his GA meetings.

But by committing to his treatment, and revisiting some family issues he had previously suppressed, he gradually learned to conquer his addiction.

It's seven and a half years since he turned his back on that life. There have been no relapses, and he's still going well at 39. But he knows he has to continue with his recovery programme.

His three meetings per week, combined with his work as a counsellor for the Cuan Mhuire Addiction Treatment Centre in Newry, and his ongoing love for the GAA are what enable him to maintain a balance in his life.

He will forever be an addict and his work as a counsellor is a constant reminder of that.

'We've very short memories because we forget the losses that we had and go again. If we forget where we came from or where we were, we'd be gone back there straight away. You listen to fellas coming into the room that are raw and that brings you back to where you were.

'If you weren't going three days a week, you'd forget and go back.

'Your addiction will tell you, 'Sure you weren't that bad, you can have one bet.' And once you've one bet, you're gone. I do a relapse prevention group in Gamblers Anonymous. They all say they stopped coming in and went for one bet and did even more damage the next time.'

He has cleared his debts and repaired the damage he caused while suffering from the addiction, but some aspects of his former life cannot be restored.

'It's great to have the relationship with them [his family] and see them whenever I like, but I still can't put them to bed,' says O'Connor.

'I get invited back out for Christmas Day and I do be over the moon but then at six o'clock, I have to go home crying to myself that I can't live with them.'

When he first linked up with the Dublin Ladies footballers at the start of the 2017 campaign, the players were hurting from their three previous All-Ireland final defeats. O'Connor, too, was carrying some hurt of his own.

Together they climbed the mountain, peaking on that glorious September Sunday with victory over Mayo. O'Connor feels that they helped each other in overcoming that past and is grateful to them for being part of his recovery.

'They don't realise how much they've helped me this year getting to where I got through sport. Sport has helped me big time.

'The hurt they've had has brought them on to this level, the same as me. I don't think I've had a better year than this year with getting involved with the Ladies.

'The thing about a gambler is they never finish things, they only do half things. I went to Cuan Mhuire two years ago to be a counsellor. I never thought I'd get over the finish line. To be able to bring my mother and the kids down to Cuan Mhuire for my graduation, the All-Ireland, the way I'm able to deal with things now, I'm getting stronger and stronger all the time.'

—

SEVEN

THE DAY KATIE TAYLOR TOOK ON THE BOYS OF BALLYFERMOT

—

EOIN O'CALLAGHAN | 13 JANUARY

AS SOON AS he answers the phone, Kenny Hammond is laughing.

He knows why I'm calling.

'How are you keeping?' I ask.

'Not too bad now, not too bad,' he says.

'But I'd rather there wasn't a video going around of me being kicked by a girl!'

Over the past week, Hammond has unwittingly turned into something of a viral sensation.

Back in the late-1990s, he was part of an excellent Cherry Orchard underage side.

Alongside him in the team were the likes of future Republic of Ireland international Stephen Quinn and Kilmarnock's Gary Dicker. Shane McFaul cut his professional teeth at Notts County and subsequently used his football as a passport by playing on three different continents. There was also Paul Byrne and Derek Doyle, who would both go on to have solid careers in the League of Ireland.

Their formative football education came in Ballyfermot and the countless days and nights spent in The Lawns – the collection of pitches in Le Fanu Park, just off the main road.

By 1998, the group — then Under-12 — were beginning to blossom and would regularly hand out thumpings to all and sundry.

'We were the kings of schoolboy up until Under-16s,' Hammond remembers.

'I think we won the All-Ireland in '98. And we won the league three or four times as we made our way through the different age-groups. We did the double one year. We won the Solar cup over in Liverpool at one stage. We had a nice little team there, so we did.'

One Saturday morning, Hammond and his team-mates were in cup action and hosted Wicklow side Newtown Juniors at their home patch.

Twenty years later and he can still recall the finer details of the game and for good reason.

That was the day he was left embarrassed by Katie Taylor.

'In the warm-up, we'd seen a girl on their team,' he says.

'Obviously we didn't know it was Katie at the time but we were all saying — laughing — 'Ah, who's gonna get stung with the girl?' And, sure as shit, when we lined up there she was on the right wing and I thought, 'You're kidding me?''

Hammond was the Orchard's left-sided midfielder and was unsettled by the prospect of taking on a girl.

'When you come up against a girl in sport you're a bit taken aback,' he admits.

'It was very unusual. That was the only time we had ever experienced it.'

As soon as the game kicked off, the Orchard wanted to test

Taylor's mettle. But Hammond quickly found out that she was well able to look after herself. This was no shrinking violet.

'I remember the boys saying, 'Get it out to Kenny, get it out to Kenny — it's only a girl,' y'know?' Hammond says.

'But she was dirty. She was dirty. Very dirty.'

He remains exasperated by how much of a nuisance she was.

'She was at me all game,' he continues.

'The lads got a great kick out of it. They kept on passing to me and saying, 'Let his girlfriend kick him again.''

Taylor clattered Hammond a few times during the game. But, unluckily for him, someone in the crowd brought a video camera along. And, over two decades later, a grainy clip surfaced online.

Hugging the left touchline, Hammond — in the Orchard white — uses his pace to whip around the outside of Taylor. But as he looks to race clear, he's caught from behind by a crunching challenge and put on his arse.

The ball was there (we think).

Taylor has seen the clip and, through a mutual friend, passes on the message that she definitely got the ball.

Perhaps inevitably, Hammond has a slightly different recollection and maintains that he was on the receiving end of a hatchet job.

'It's just as well they only caught the one tackle on camera because she was like that for the whole thing!' he says.

I press him for more details.

'It was just dirty stuff. She'd be pulling you, kicking you. Just dirty. At one stage I got a free-kick and even the ref came over to me and said, 'Jesus, she's giving you an awful time, isn't she?' And I was like, 'Well, are you going to fucking book her?' And he just shakes his head and says, 'No, no — I'm not going to book her.' So I says, 'Cheers for that, mate' and that was it. She got away with fucking murder. Absolute murder!

'Even at half-time, we might've been a few goals up and our manager was telling everyone to knock the ball out to me so I could get kicked again. She shouldn't have lasted the 60 minutes, or however long we were playing for. She should've got her marching orders. And another thing... she was as quiet as a mouse. I don't even think I heard her talking. She just kicked!

'But it's some nice footage to have, isn't it?'

Taylor's footballing prowess has been completely overshadowed by her achievements in the ring but she easily could've been a professional player.

Around the same time that she was taking chunks out of Kenny Hammond, she was being crowned Wicklow's 'Schoolboy' of the Year. Shortly after, she made the county's Kennedy Cup team.

She was still in her early teens when she was called up to the Republic of Ireland Under-17 squad, her physicality — honed by her boxing training — ensuring she could mix it with older girls. At the 2004 FAI Awards, she was named Under-19 Women's Player of the Year. The following year, as a crucial ingredient in the Peamount side, she lost a Cup final to Dundalk. Boxing commitments ensured she missed St Catherine's appearance in the 2009 decider but the following year, with her focus beginning to move away from football entirely, she still managed to be part of the Peamount squad as they secured a domestic treble. A first senior call-up arrived when she was just 16 and she'd go on to win 19 caps.

All in all, not a bad return.

Hammond is quick to point out that despite her being a nuisance during their encounter, her wider skill-set was undeniable.

'She was the best player they had by a mile — that's no disrespect to the lads. But she was half-decent. She could play a bit of ball. And she was up against a good Orchard team. She raised her game when she came up against the big boys. It was The Lawns in Ballyer — not an easy place to come and play either. You could only have respect for her.

'They didn't have much of the ball but when she did have it she was decent. She could pick a pass and dribble away. But we were a good side so it was hard for her at the same time. All I know is I got plenty of grief over her... me 'girlfriend'.'

The Orchard, as expected, won handily that morning. But 'the girl' had made quite the impact, as evidenced by the reaction she got when it was all over.

'There were handshakes all around at full-time,' Hammond says.

'Every single one of our lads went over to her, even our manager. It was inspirational, wasn't it? Seeing a girl there playing a bit of ball. There should be more of it, really.'

Hammond put up with the stick for quite a few years and then everyone moved on. Until his father — who keeps a casual eye on women's boxing — recognised 'rising star' Katie Taylor from somewhere.

He just couldn't quite put his finger on how he knew her.

'Me Da twigged it, eventually,' Hammond says.

'He gave me grief over that game for a long while. And my younger sister did some boxing and me Da follows it a bit. And he said to me, 'I'm sure it was that Katie Taylor that kicked you that day up in The Lawns.' And I said to him, 'No, it's not.' But one of the team-mates from that day — Paul Byrne — well, his Da would've taped a lot of our games and then another team-mate — Derek Kavanagh — got that clip, stuck it up on the football Facebook page he runs and, sure as shit, there I am. So cheers for that, Derek.'

'I still get stick off me Da to this day. We'll be out having a pint or two and he'll start off, 'Remember that girl...', and I'll say, 'It wasn't just any girl — it was Katie Taylor."

Anytime he watches her now, Hammond can still see the young girl from that day in The Lawns. The grit, the desire, the fight, the talent.

'At least she's allowed use her fists now,' he says, with another laugh.

'Fair play to her. Inspirational to women... and men. I have so much time for her.'

I attempt to reassure him about the video clip. It could, after all, have been Taylor sticking the ball through Hammond's legs and jinking past him.

'You're right — that would've been a lot worse. Getting nutmegged by Katie Taylor? Me bollix. At least the boys got great craic out of it. Not a bit of pity did I get from anyone when a girl was kicking me.'

Hammond's career came to a premature end because of injury. He picked up three underage caps for his country and had stints with Nottingham Forest, Notts County and Burnley but was done by the age of 20.

'It was a bad hip injury that did me in the end,' he says.

'I don't know if Katie had a part to play in that!'

Now a plumber and based in Clondalkin, he has not moved too far away from Ballyer. Life is good. The father to two boys, he'll tell them the story soon enough.

'It's something to talk to them about in the future, isn't it?' he says.

'When we see Katie with her world titles: 'See her? She kicked the shit outta me!"

EIGHT

'I LOOK DOWN THE BACK OF THE BUS AND THERE'S CLAW, FAG IN HIS MOUTH, PUFFING AWAY'

—

MURRAY KINSELLA | 13 JUNE

THERE WERE MANY times in his first few weeks with Munster when John Langford wondered what he had let himself in for.

There was the fishing trip with Dominic Crotty, Brian O'Brien and David Corkery where, after a collective bout of seasickness, they caught plenty of mackerel and Langford was explaining how smoking their catch would be the best option when they were back on dry land.

The captain of the boat they had rented disagreed, insisted raw was best and bit the head off one of the mackerel moments after it had been reeled in.

There was the unforgettably rough first landing into Shannon airport, the plane bouncing back up off the runway before thumping down permanently, at which the pilot announced, 'Welcome to Shannon, two landings for the price of one.'

There was the time Munster were in Kilkee for a training camp and when they went on an orienteering trip, Langford pointed out that he was carrying an ankle injury and might have to sit it out.

Declan Kidney's response: 'That's alright, if you come back we know the ankle is alright. If you don't come back, we know you won't be right to play.' Langford completed the course with flying colours.

And then there was Peter Clohessy, known to one and all simply as 'Claw'.

Sitting in Brisbane before Ireland's first Test against the Wallabies, Langford smiles and laughs often as he recalls his three years with Munster from 1999 onwards — during which time he had a major influence on the province's progress.

With him on the trip to Brisbane from their home in Sydney is his 18-year-old son, Connor, who was born in Limerick.

Langford and his wife, Nicole — who also have two daughters, 15-year-old Olivia and 10-year-old Anna — remain in close contact with the lifelong friends they made in Munster but in those early days, the Australian second row had a few reality checks after coming from the extremely professional Brumbies set-up.

'We were in Wales for a warm-up match and we hopped on the bus and we're heading down the road,' recalls Langford.

'A few guys are playing cards and I suddenly think, 'I can smell cigarette smoke.' I was just thinking, 'How rude of the bus driver, we're going to play a match and he's smoking.'

'But then I look down the back of the bus and there's Claw, fag in his mouth, puffing away on the way to the game. I'm thinking, 'What have I got myself into?''

Isa Nacewa's recent retirement restarted the debate about the greatest ever import into Irish rugby and many would put Langford's name forward for that title.

While the Australian lock was gone by the time Munster finally reached their holy grail of Heineken Cup success in 2006, his influence on the province's professionalism and training approach has been stressed by virtually everyone who was part of the journey to that long-awaited European trophy.

The funny thing is that Langford very nearly ended up being a Leinster player.

He had lost his starting spot at the Brumbies to Justin Harrison when he decided to cash in and look for a club in the UK or France, but the lack of a European passport made things more difficult.

A coach of his at the Brumbies, Jake Howard, suggested looking in Ireland and Langford made contact with former Leinster Branch and IRFU president Peter Boyle.

'I started to talk to Boyler and was looking, believe it or not, to play for Leinster,' says Langford.

'We had agreed on an amount, nothing like what they get paid now — I nearly fell over when I heard what some of the second rowers get now — but I had agreed terms and when people asked me where I was going, I said 'I'm going to Leinster."

But all of a sudden, the communication from Leinster stopped and two weeks passed before Langford got in touch with Boyle, who informed him that the IRFU had decided only Irish players who were contracted in the country could go to the 1999 World Cup.

Malcolm O'Kelly returned to Leinster from London Irish and the second-row spot that was meant to be Langford's was gone.

Boyle recommended giving Munster a call and when Langford came to London to play for the Barbarians, he met the province's manager, Brian O'Brien, and assistant coach, Niall

O'Donovan — who is still involved today as team manager.

'I'll never forget when I put my hand out to meet Briano and he's just grabbed me on my tummy and had a squeeze and gone, 'That's alright," says 49-year-old Langford.

Langford had a good game for the Barbarians and flew on to meet Munster boss Declan Kidney in Limerick, where he had his first experience of the now-London Irish director of rugby's ability to chat incessantly around rugby.

'It was supposed to be half an hour but it went for an hour and a half, with Deccie doing all the talking.

'I actually remember back then that it was quite expensive to make calls on mobile phones in Ireland and there was a way of doing it where you could add another digit to the number and it would ring straight through to the voicemail, bypass the phone.

'Because Deccie would talk for an hour and you had to pay for the call, ROG used to ring straight through to the voicemail and say 'Declan, I tried to call you."

Langford was 30 when he signed for Munster but the fact that he had taken up rugby relatively late probably contributed to him still being in incredibly good condition.

A native of Wagga Wagga, situated between Sydney and Melbourne, Langford didn't know much about rugby union as he grew up in a city where Aussie Rules and rugby league were dominant.

He was a cross-country runner in his later school years and it wasn't until he was studying engineering at Sydney University that he was finally convinced to give rugby a go, being drafted into their fifth-grade team when they were short on numbers.

'I remember the boys trying to explain the rules to me on the way to the game, but they forgot to tell me you couldn't trip and this guy got away on me, so I threw up my leg and tripped him.

'All these guys from the opposition are trying to punch me all of a sudden.'

Even without any idea of what was going on, Langford loved the physicality and competitiveness, going on to play for the university's Under-21 side and rapidly developing into an excellent, athletic second row.

He played for New South Wales before a switch to NSW Country allowed him to feature in games against nations like South Africa and Wales on their tours of Australia, while he captained Australian Universities in 1993 and played for the Emerging Wallabies on a tour of South Africa in 1994.

Rugby was still amateur at that stage, of course, and Langford had gone into a job as an engineer in railway construction after college, a job he is still doing now.

But professionalism was on the way and Langford's impressive form for the Gordon club convinced Brumbies coach Rod Macqueen to give him a call ahead of the inaugural Super Rugby season in 1996.

With the starting salary matching his earnings in engineering, Langford jumped at the chance of becoming a foundation member of the Brumbies and was part of an excellent team that went on to reach the 1997 Super Rugby final, alongside the likes of Joe Roff, George Gregan, Stephen Larkham, Ewen McKenzie and Owen Finegan.

Langford earned Wallabies selection in 1996 and 1997, winning four caps against New Zealand, South Africa, England and Scotland but by 1999, with Eddie Jones by then in charge of the Brumbies, the second row was looking for a new adventure outside Australia. Munster proved to be his new home.

'I felt I still had some good years in me,' says Langford. 'I felt there was a bit of an expectation in Australia that you get to 30 and you're too old, but I felt I had something to prove.'

Though his new team-mate Anthony Foley gave Langford a bit of a scare at the very beginning, his level of fitness made a big impression at Munster.

The Australian has been consistently credited with bringing about far greater training standards and improved strength and conditioning in Munster, which played a vital role in their eventual rise to European success.

'I remember one of the first sessions down at UL and I lined up beside Axel for a sprint test and I was thinking, 'This fat bastard, I'll beat him easy," says Langford.

'Fergal O'Callaghan, our strength and conditioning coach, blew the whistle and Axel was about two yards in front of me before I'd even twitched. He was deceptively quick off the mark.

'But we did the 3k run and I lapped John Hayes on about the second lap! I was one of the fittest guys back home and that was probably the difference with me, I could go all game.

'I think the guys in Munster thought everyone in Australia was like that so it might have been a wake-up call for them that way.

'I'd heard stories about when it first turned professional and they said, 'Right, train for eight hours a day,' and they'd flog the boys. Eight hours a day training and you'd try to play at the weekend but they'd be wrecked and they were losing.'

Munster's expectations needed to be lifted too.

'We had this session in one of the theatres down in UL and the legend Dave Mahedy [now UL's director of sport and recreation] was there with us, so we're sitting there as a squad and the question comes up, 'Who thinks we can win the Heineken Cup this year?'

'I put my hand up, Woody [Keith Wood] put his hand up

and one other person. They're asking can we go through the season undefeated and the three same blokes put their hand up. I was thinking, 'Why not? What games are we planning to lose?'

'The same question was asked the next year and every hand in the room went up. I wish I had a video of that.'

Off the pitch, Nicole also had an influence.

'She would come to all the functions because that's what we did at the Brumbies,' explains Langford.

'I think she made a change to a few things in Munster in terms of getting the wives and girlfriends to come to post-match functions and things like that. You look back and think, 'How was it not always like that?' It was important.'

While Munster's approach to training changed, with Langford's experiences with the Brumbies proving important, he also learned plenty from playing with his club side, Shannon, in the AIL and in the red jersey of Munster.

'Even from the first match for Shannon, I could see these guys were working themselves up into a frenzy to play. I went up to Geoff Moylan, the coach, and said, 'This seems a bit wrong, why aren't we focusing?'

'We used to do that in the Brumbies, focusing on each bit of play, like the kickoff, focusing on all that. After a couple of weeks playing for Shannon, I gave up.

'The passion of the players was something I'd never experienced before and I sort of ended up mirroring it. It was very powerful running onto the pitch with that passion, whereas in the Brumbies it wasn't this same raw passion, it was more technical. When you blend the passion with the right skills, that's when you get the results.'

Munster certainly began to click and Kidney's side won

five of their six pool games in the Heineken Cup — including a stunning win away to Saracens — before beating Stade Français in the quarter-finals and pulling off their famous 31-25 win away to Toulouse in the semi-finals.

Suddenly, Kidney's men found themselves in the 2000 Heineken Cup final and the agony of that 9-8 defeat to Northampton lives on to this day.

Langford, having laughed through our interview, sighs and ruefully shakes his head when it comes up.

'My mate here in Brisbane, Tony Rees, won a Heineken Cup with Brive in 1997 and he was saying they had a 20-year reunion for that team. We were just a couple of points shy of that. It was heartbreaking, there were tears from everyone.

'A lot of our games were won with the kicks ROG got. I'll never forget at Twickenham the day before at our captain's walkthrough, Ronan was kicking and it was very blustery. He wasn't listening probably but I remembering saying to him to watch the wind.

'We got a penalty kick towards the end of the game and I was behind Ronan, it was almost exactly where I'd seen him kicking the day before and it was the same blustery wind. I was right behind and the kick started well but just faded to the left. It was heartbreaking.

'I don't blame him for that at all because we wouldn't have got to where we got without ROG; he won us so many games with his kicking.

'I ran into Paul Grayson [who kicked Northampton's nine points that day in Twickenham] at a Legends match in 2013. I saw him at the after-match function and I could have throttled him for his kicks that day.'

Though he only signed on for one year at a time, Kidney

managed to convince Langford and Nicole to stay on for three seasons before they returned home to Australia.

By the time Langford was getting set to move on, the next great Munster second row, Paul O'Connell, was emerging.

'Paulie came onto the scene at that time and I remember playing against him at the Cookies, he made a big impression,' says Langford.

For his part, O'Connell was impressed by the Australian.

'Langford was a superstar of a second row,' says O'Connell in his book, 'The Battle'. 'If it wasn't for John Eales, he'd probably have won fifty caps for the Wallabies.'

Though Munster couldn't get over the line in his time there, Langford is grateful to have played with legends like Clohessy, Alan Quinlan, David Wallace, Hayes, O'Gara, Peter Stringer, 'Dutchy' Holland, Mike Mullins, Crotty, Anthony Horgan and John Kelly.

Langford formed a great connection with hooker Wood, which proved important in that march to the 2000 final.

'Woody was back that year, what a player,' says Langford. 'You talk about people being 100% all the time, he was 300% into everything, so to have Woody there was great.

'It was something that just clicked between us in training. We worked very well together and it was a great combo. Frankie Sheahan stepped in after and continued that.

'I had a go at Woody the other day because Munster played Ireland twice in my time, even before the World Cup in 1999 we beat them down in Musgrave Park. All the fellas who didn't get picked were angry. Woody was telling the story of how Axel nearly cut him in half!'

Mick Galwey was the captain of the team and Langford's second-row partner.

'He was great, the respect he got,' says the Australian. 'We had a dinner down in Charleville once. I was asked to speak and I told a few home truths about Gaillimh and it wasn't complimentary, but I was just joking obviously.

'Well, I thought they were going to bloody lynch me, they didn't like me talking poorly of him! He was up there on a pedestal and I didn't think I'd get out of there alive. He was a great captain and he would give everything and get stuck in.'

And then there was the great Axel, a dear friend of Langford's, their bond built up during times they shared on the pitch, the laughs they had off it, the chats during their car trips from Limerick to Cork and back for training, with Marcus Horan and Colm McMahon part of their crew too.

Langford's most recent visit to Ireland was a desperately sad one as he attended Foley's funeral in Killaloe in 2016.

Langford explains that his son Connor's Irish godparents are Axel and Olive Foley, a sign of the connection between the two families.

'Axel used to advise me which journalist I could talk to and who not to talk to,' says Langford with a smile as our chat draws to a conclusion.

'Axel had a rugby head on his shoulders. He could just see things I couldn't and he could play. I remember him winning the pizzas for life in Domino's for his three tries [against Biarritz in 2001] and there was no better man for it, even though he said he didn't eat that many.

'We miss him dearly.'

NINE

TEENAGE KICKS: FROM KILDARE GAA TO THE PREMIER LEAGUE

—

BEN BLAKE | 14 APRIL

'HE WAS JUST *one of those all-rounders. If he was playing chess, he would have been good at that as well.'*

Conor Masterson is a name you will probably have heard plenty about in recent weeks.

At just 19, the Kildare-born defender appears to be on the verge of a first-team debut for Premier League giants Liverpool, having been named on the bench for games against Manchester City and Everton this month.

If he is handed his senior bow by Jurgen Klopp, it will be the result of years of work, dedication and sacrifice by a player who signed a €1 million contract with the Reds from Lucan United back in 2012.

However, we could quite easily have been watching the teenager line out in the white of Kildare GAA, as he was an extremely talented Gaelic footballer before choosing to concentrate on soccer.

'Conor was a top-class footballer,' Gerry Kearns, who coached Masterson at his local club Celbridge between the ages of six and 14, told *The42* this week. 'I would have seen him play soccer, and he was even more effective as a Gaelic footballer.

'He was a lovely lad to work with. He had great application and he was confident but, whereas some kids at that age might be a bit cocky, he was never that way.'

A rangy midfielder with good height and the technical ability to play anywhere on the field, Kearns remains adamant that Masterson would have been destined to play inter-county football for the Lilywhites had he not opted to pack it in.

'There's no doubt he would have made it to the top,' says Kearns. 'That age group was fairly strong, but in Kildare, he would have been the top player by a good bit.

'I don't think there was any question about it. There was no one from that year that could have stood side-by-side with him.'

If that wasn't impressive enough, he also tried his hand at the small ball.

'Conor was fantastic in the hurling as well,' he adds. 'He wouldn't have been as prolific, as he didn't have the time to perfect the skillset because he was always busy. He was nearly training professionally with Lucan at that stage, then he had football training with us and county sessions too.'

According to Kearns, the entire club are hugely proud of how Masterson has developed and they continue to follow his progress closely.

'For any young fella who has the chance of playing professional sport, you will always say best of luck to them. If it was a case that Celbridge had €200 million, I'd buy him in the morning.

'It's great for a fella to go and make career for himself, and hopefully everything will work out for him. He has the application and he just needs a bit of luck to get a start and he'll go on from there.

'Everybody down here is extremely proud of him. We would have had Paddy Brophy, who went off to the AFL [Australian Football League] for two years. He's back but it's great for any of them as, unfortunately, we don't have that option in the GAA.'

Conor's only football club prior to the dream move to Liverpool was Lucan United. His father, Ciarán, had brought him down at an early age and he ended up agreeing to take charge of the team when they were in need of a manager.

With more than three decades' experience coaching Palmerstown Rangers and Dublin Bus, he set about building a strong side that would play in the notoriously competitive Dublin District Schoolboy League (DDSL) Premier, and Lucan would go on to reach an All-Ireland final and win a Dublin Cup.

That helped the club keep hold of its biggest assets instead of losing them to the league's heavyweights likes St Kevin's Boys and Cherry Orchard. Masterson was one of 10 Lucan team-mates to earn underage international caps, with the likes of goalkeeper Mark Travers joining Bournemouth, Brandon Payne moving to Celtic, Sean Whelan signing for Preston North End and Cristian Magerusan ending up at Bohemians.

Confident in his own ability and always eager to learn, his former coach John Doyle says Conor was an absolute joy to work with.

'You could see straight off that he had talent, but lots of kids have talent,' Doyle remembers. 'The difference with Conor was that he worked really hard, even from a young age. He wanted to do extra training and he would always be at the top of the session when we were doing drills.

'He wouldn't be doing things by half, no matter what it was. It was full on and the work ethic was there. It helps a lot that he is very clever. He's a studious boy and he would have done well in his Leaving Cert.

'The technical ability came very quickly and he grew to a good height early on. But he wasn't your typical clumsy, tall lad who would win the day with physicality. He was clever and he always tried to play football.

'He's a good leader too and he captained those teams growing up. He knows how to deal with other players. He wasn't a shouter, but he gets to know players and what makes them tick.

'We've some good coaches in the club. Alan McGovern would have been one of his early mentors. He worked with the FAI and knew his stuff inside out. Alan would be going through things with the players and Conor would pick it up straight away. He was a sponge.

'Outside the club, he would work extremely hard and do his own stuff to get fitter and stronger. He didn't just depend on Lucan United and he would be away doing his own bit out of season.

'There are so many talented kids out there but it's following it up with the work that gets you there.'

As well as learning from coaches like Doyle, McGovern and his father Ciarán, Ger Desmond was another figure who had a big influence on Masterson's development.

Now a centre-half by trade, the Ireland Under-19 international featured in various positions growing up.

'In those days, he probably played more up front than he

did at the back, but he chopped and changed,' adds Doyle. 'He might revert back to centre-half for a big game if we needed him.

'It depended on the personnel. If we felt we were strong at the back, he would then go and play up front and he scored a lot of goals. He could play in midfield too — pretty much anywhere. He had a very good footballing brain from an early age.'

Masterson enjoyed trials with several of the top clubs and there were contract offers on the table from Manchester United and Man City, but Liverpool felt right. Kenny Dalglish had welcomed him with open arms on a visit to Merseyside and Conor became the first signing under Brendan Rodgers — the deal was wrapped up the morning that Fabio Borini.

The defender trained with the first-team squad during the Rodgers era at just 16, but it is under Klopp that Masterson has featured in matchday squads at senior level.

He may be with one of the top clubs in English football, but Masterson hasn't forgotten his roots and he can often be found back at Lucan United's training ground during visits home to Ireland.

'He's very humble about the club and he will always tell people Lucan got him where he is,' reveals Doyle. 'He comes back all the time. Whenever he's home, he is up at our academy. He has trained with our first team when he's been here too.

'I do think he's going to be a player. Liverpool are a top club and it's very difficult for an Irish player to get in, but he will do everything possible to succeed and if he does, I think he will prove himself. But if the cards don't fall right for him, he'll go somewhere else and be a success.'

—

TEN

SILVER SATURDAY AS IRELAND'S YOUNG SPRINTERS TAKE ON THE WORLD

—

EMMA DUFFY | 10 SEPTEMBER

THE FIRST LEG is hugely important. They all are, of course, but the first leg determines the staggers and like anything, a good start is half the battle.

Sitting in the blocks, waiting for the gun to go, 101 different things could run through an athlete's mind.

But not for Molly Scott. Not on this day.

Saturday, 14 July 2018. Tampere, Finland. The IAAF World Under-20 Championships. The women's 4x100m final.

The day that four young women won a world sprint silver for Ireland.

'Everything was kind of quiet,' Scott recalls. Spaced out in her own little world, she just knew she had a job to do.

That calmness flowed from their time together in the call room. Scott and her three Irish team-mates, Gina Akpe-Moses, Ciara Neville and Patience Jumbo-Gula, sat quietly away from the hype, heroes-in-waiting.

'I think we were all individually really nervous but we were acting calm even though we were kind of dying on the inside,' Scott continues.

'It's a different type of pressure, not individual. If I messed up, I messed up for everybody. I knew I had to get it right. I think we all knew we did, and we knew we would.'

There was some dancing done in that call-room and plenty of positive vibes, she smiles, epitomising the spirit and team bond between this group of rising stars. Counting down to the biggest moment of their young careers, they never stopped enjoying themselves.

'Once you step out and walk down, it gets easier,' she adds.

Lagos-born Akpe-Moses echoes her words. 'We were all really, really chilled,' she says. 'In previous years, we put a lot of pressure on ourselves before and messed up a little bit.

'This year we just kept a level head and kept calm, we just wanted to do the job. It was less thought and more action. We didn't have to stress out, we didn't have to be nervous, we just had to replicate what we did in the heat.

'It wasn't an impossible task. We knew we could do it again.'

Again.

The dream of medals had become reality, just fingertips away, with a brilliant qualifying run. Ireland's time of 44.27 was comfortably good enough to win the second of the two heats, and the second-fastest time overall with only Germany, the eventual world champions, clocking faster.

But the team, coached by Karen Kirk, failed to make it through the race unscathed. Fifteen-year-old sensation Rhasidat Adeleke — who had won 200 metre gold at the European Under-18 Championships in Hungary just five days prior — flew around the bends in the third leg of the heats and felt her hamstring go while doing so.

Adeleke powered on to get the baton safely to Jumbo-Gula, and now that's just what her team-mates would have to do: power on for her. Neville would slot in to run the third leg of the final in her place, and it would be as you were. Onto the big one. Where they wanted to be.

'I didn't think of anything,' says Scott, on the blocks. 'That's when you run your best race, when you get into the blocks and nothing goes through your head because you're calm.'

This was it. Showtime.

Marks... set... BAM.

Out of the blocks fast.

Everything started to plan in lane five. You'd often think, in retrospect, that it's all a blur for the athlete. Between the sound of the gun, the adrenaline and the chase to zone two, it's over in a flash. But Scott has some clear recollections.

'I remember it all,' she continues. 'Obviously the girl outside me, that's always the person I'm aiming to catch for the majority of the leg. It was 100%, give it everything I had.

'When I get around the corner, it's scary because I can't see Gina when I'm running into her. I'm almost in the zone by the time I do.'

Baton in the right hand, check. In the zone, check. Gina's hand is there, check. Just get the baton into it safely and she'll take it from there.

By the time Scott arrived at full tilt, Akpe-Moses was at ease again after a stressful few minutes before the gun sounded.

When she arrived down to zone two, there was no tape to be found for the runners' markings. It was a key part of her preparation: focus, get the tape, do the markings. Of optimum importance for the baton change, but also a welcome distraction from the hustle and bustle around her.

'It was quite hectic, I'm not going to lie,' she admits.

'I was honestly thinking, 'I'm not running. They can start the gun but I will not move because if there's no tape, I don't know where I'm going to go off or where Molly's going to hit the mark.' I was getting really pissed off, I was getting so frustrated.

'If Molly went off, I wouldn't have ran the race. I would have sat there on the track and not done anything — until I got my tape!'

Luckily enough, it didn't come to that and everything was in order by the time Scott powered around the bend. The first and second leg duo had been in this situation many, many times before so they knew they could pull the changeover off and get on with it.

'Our changeover is always pretty good,' Akpe-Moses continues. 'We've been through it together for so many years. We've never, ever had a bad changeover because we're just so used to each other. I haven't even got to hear her say, 'Hand,' I just know. I never worry with her.'

'It was pretty outstretched but in a good way,' Scott adds.

Smooth, steady, moving on. Baton in hand, Akpe-Moses rocketed up the back straight. 'Run, Gina, Run,' is all she thought to herself as she made a beeline for Neville.

'I was just chasing the German girl outside of me. They were our only proper competition in the final because they ran the quickest time in the heats. I was aiming for her, just chasing her the whole time.'

All eyes on the changeover, and on the next in line.

Two days earlier, Neville had been in the stands watching on, most definitely more nervous than she was before running.

'I was shaking, I was sweating,' she laughs.

As she walked to take her place in zone three and wait for the starter's gun, the nerves were of a different kind, and a little less shaky, luckily. This time, things were in her control.

'It was nerve-wracking, it was really hot as well. We kept rubbing our hands off our kit to make sure they weren't sweaty or whatever.'

En route to her destination, she walked past some Irish supporters. A few cheers — 'Best of luck, Ciara' — and no shortage of green, but she had to shut it all out. Head down, walk on.

There was no apprehension from Neville. It was just like any other race. She hadn't really ran the third leg much in competition before, she admits, but everything had been practiced meticulously in training. Any one of the four could run in any position.

The team knew they'd be without Adeleke from Friday night so there was no last-minute drama in that sense. They trusted one another to go out and do their job, each confident in their own abilities and in their team-mates.

'She was just tearing down the back straight,' Neville recalls as she watched the onslaught of the second leg runners. 'I was like, 'Right, just get the baton and run as fast as you can and get it into Patience's hand."

There were a few Irish fans at the zone, the volume turning up a few notches as the Girls in Green grew more and more into the race. Scott, on the other hand, says she couldn't watch. Neville hadn't ran the third leg a whole lot before. She wasn't overly used to getting the baton in her right hand. But getting it done was all that mattered.

And Akpe-Moses was fully aware of that too.

'It was a bit tricky to get it in. We did get it in, we were always going to. It wasn't that smooth, it could have been better, we could have gotten more out of it.

'We made so many mistakes in the final but I think because we were so calm and experienced as well, we were able to handle it with such ease. If that was any other team, I guarantee you the baton would have dropped.

'If we were a younger team or if we were less experienced, I know for a fact the baton could have dropped so easy, but we just kept calm.'

Neville knew it was far from perfect too, but they got through it and off she went, her legs moving as fast as they possibly could. The chase was well and truly on.

'I just took the baton and literally attacked the bend, kept running until I got it into Patience's hand.'

As Neville rounded the bend from lane five, the teams were all still fairly staggered. Ireland were in fourth position with France on the outside and Switzerland next in lane seven but, as expected, it was Germany who had the edge as they all rounded the corner for the final changeover.

Now everything rested on one moment of coordination. The heartbreak, the shortcomings, the fourth-placed finishes could all be erased with one final changeover and a dash to the finish line. Scott was watching on, as was Akpe-Moses. Both powerless, they had done all they could. It was out of their hands.

It was down to the final two. This was it: from Neville's right hand to Jumbo-Gula's left and then up that home straight like the hammers of hell.

Again, the pass could have been cleaner.

'Our changeover was a little bit messy but we still got it

into her [Jumbo-Gula's] hand safely,' Neville continues. 'She literally took it and she knew she had to run as fast as she could.

'When I passed over the baton, I think I stopped for like a split second and then I just ran down the home straight behind her, shouting at her.'

There was a sense of sheer relief from the sea of green around the stadium when Jumbo-Gula had the baton firmly — and securely — in her left hand.

'I knew once Patience got away and got the baton in her hand she was fine,' their coach Karen Kirk told *The42* shortly after the team's return to home soil.

'Once Patience got the baton in her hand, it was then that I started to shout because I knew all of the changeovers were done and there was nothing more I could do.'

Jumbo-Gula had watched the other three legs closely, calm rather than nervous. The atmosphere, the support, the buzz was unreal, she recalls, but she didn't get too caught up in it. As Neville came into view, she braced herself.

'I could see where Ciara was, I think we were coming fourth or third, I'm not sure,' Jumbo-Gula begins.

'The Great Britain girl was to my left and the German girl was to my right, so I was trying really hard to catch them.

'Our changeover was really bad. I wanted the baton as soon as possible because I knew the Germans were going to be gone, and that was our main target: to beat the Germans.

'It was just a bit slow because Ciara has never passed the baton to me. It was the first time, so it was a big risk, but it was ok.

'When I got the baton, I was sprinting really hard and I could see that I was passing the Great Britain girl, and I could see myself getting to the German girl.'

She passed the Italian finisher too in a phenomenal kick. The memories come thicker and faster the more she describes her closing leg.

'All I remember is people screaming, the crowd screaming. I remember gritting my teeth and trying really, really hard. And then when I could see myself come up from fourth to third, to second, I was like, 'OK...''

But then the ending came, and it was all over. Just like that.

'The finish line was just there,' she sighs with a sense that maybe, just maybe, if there were just a few more metres in the race, it could have been gold.

'We were so close but we're still happy that we got a medal. I can't even describe it. It was a shock. After I crossed the finish line, I didn't celebrate. I was just waiting for our country's name to come up on the board. I wasn't sure.

'Then when it came up, I wanted to faint. It was unreal. I'll never forget that.'

Just like Jumbo-Gula, Scott, Akpe-Moses and Neville stood, watching, waiting until the standings flashed up on the board. And there it was.

Ireland. 43.90. National Under-20 record. World silver medallists.

After chasing her down the home straight, Neville was first to reach Jumbo-Gula at the line.

They held hands, embraced and screamed their heads off as they waited for Scott and Akpe-Moses to join the party.

'It was actually almost a blur,' Neville smiles. 'We just couldn't believe it.

'We were all screaming. Patience was crying. It was absolutely amazing, we couldn't get over it. We just saw all the Irish fans coming down to the gate, we all ran over and they were giving us flags and hugs and everything. It was amazing.'

'It was crazy,' Scott echoes her sentiments. 'We were all screaming and shouting, it was so good. It was pretty overwhelming.

'There was a big expectation on us too from the whole country. We didn't really think about that. I think it was just about the four of us and our coach Karen Kirk... It was about us five or six and the whole squad wanting to get a medal. We didn't really feel the pressure around us and I think that's why we got the medal.

'We enjoyed every single moment.'

Like life itself, there are always lows that go hand-in-hand with the highs. For Adeleke, watching on from the sidelines, it wasn't exactly ideal.

'Ohhh... it wasn't great,' she admits. 'I was forcing myself to act like I was okay, but I wasn't. I was devastated because I knew the girls would be able to medal and just not being able to run in the final was really devastating.'

She too is now a world silver medallist, delighted for the team-mates who went on to finish the job in her absence.

Akpe-Moses meanwhile, was the last to join the celebrations as she had the longest walk around the track. Cool as a breeze, she took it all in — well, as much of it as she could wrap her head around at the time.

'To this day, I'm not that good at understanding the depth of winning a medal and everything — even when I came first at Europeans last year, I still don't get it. It hasn't hit me. I'm like, 'Oh yeah, that happened.'

'I think what was really special was just all the fans. There was loads of people asking for pictures. It was really cute. I was like, 'Ah, people actually really care about us and wanted us to medal.' That was quite special really, the support.'

In a few years, they will all look back on the phenomenal feat and fully appreciate it no doubt, a silver success which paves the way for future gold. Irish sprinting is in the best place it's been in years, and its future is most definitely in good hands. There's a truly special crop coming through, and there's still some time to go before they reach their peak.

'It's really exciting to know that Irish sprinting has such a good future,' Akpe-Moses concludes.

'Ireland is finally getting the recognition we deserve, it's good. We came second, we're at the level. We know we can do basically almost anything.'

That they can. And that they will.

—

ELEVEN

ONE LAST GAME ON A HOSPITAL WARD FOR TWO OLD FRIENDS AND FIERCE COMPETITORS

—

KEVIN O'BRIEN | 11 NOVEMBER

MELBOURNE, 1984

Before Jim Stynes ever set foot in Australia, Garry Lyon had made his way to Ireland.

In 1984, Lyon was part of the Australia Under-17 team that travelled to play an International Rules series against Ireland. He would go on to score 426 goals in 226 AFL games for Melbourne Football Club, become the longest-serving captain in the club's history and win more All-Australian (All-Star) honours than any other Melbourne player.

But 33 years ago, Lyon was just another skinny 16-year-old with a dream. For the majority of that Under-17 Australian squad, it would be their only visit to this country. He didn't know it at the time, but it was only the beginning of a long relationship between Garry Lyon and the Irish.

'We spent five weeks there as 16-year-old boys just travelling around and playing six or seven games,' he tells *The42* from

Melbourne. 'It was magnificent.'

That September, an 18-year-old Jim Stynes from Rathfarnham helped the Dublin minors to an All-Ireland football title.

Shortly after the victory, he attended a trial in Dublin for the chance to win a scholarship with Aussie Rules outfit the Melbourne Demons. By the end of the week-long camp, Stynes was offered a contract by the Demons; two weeks later, he was sitting on a plane on his way to the other side of the world.

Within seven years, Stynes was voted the best and most dominant player in Australian Rules. But when he first landed Down Under, he couldn't have been further away from winning the famous Brownlow Medal.

'This weird-looking, pasty-skinned, fairly ugly-looking man, to be honest, arrived at training,' laughed Lyon in the 2012 documentary 'Every Heart Beats True'.

'We watched him play footy and we thought, 'This is the greatest joke of all-time.' We didn't appreciate the sort of person Jim was at that time.'

Naturally, there was a difficult bedding-in period for Stynes as he settled into an almost alien culture. He wrote in his autobiography: 'My accent was the subject of great mirth. I often had to repeat myself.

'I would get baffled looks when I referred to people as 'yer man' or 'yer woon' and some friends took great delight in tallying the different ways I used the term 'bollocks' in conversation. There was 'a load of bollocks' [nonsense], 'what a bollocks' [an idiot], 'he's made a bollocks of that' [a mess] and 'I'm bollocksed' [tired], to list just a few.'

Lyon agrees with Stynes' assessment. He reckons the Melbourne Under-19s 'thought he was a strange man when he first arrived' and they 'couldn't understand a word he said'. When he introduced himself to Stynes, Lyon told him he was from Kyabram (a small town located 200km north of Melbourne).

Stynes misunderstood Lyon's tan and thick black hair, presuming Kyabram was somewhere far away in the Australian outback. He arrived home to his boarding family that evening, and over dinner declared, 'I met my first Australian Aborigine today.' 'I got a few laughs out of that story over the years,' Stynes wrote in his book.

'He was a little older than me,' Lyon says. 'Once we advanced to senior footy, he was struggling and he couldn't really cement his spot in the team. I wouldn't say we were overly close [at the start].

'He had to go back and play at a lower level for Prahran [Melbourne's VFL team] and that's when his footy started to really blossom. He came back and by 1987 he was a part of our senior team. That's when our friendship really kicked in.

'I said many times, we didn't always see eye-to-eye, Jimmy and I. He was pretty obstinate and pig-headed and I was probably the same so we used to clash a bit. But the older and more mature I got, the greater my understanding of him and what he stood for and his values. I just loved the man.'

Lyon made his Melbourne debut in 1986 and a year later Stynes arrived on the scene. They soldiered side-by-side with the Demons up until Stynes retired in 1998 and became very close friends.

Tom Brady and LeBron James have made public their age-defying practices and unique training methods. But back in the 1990s, Jim Stynes was the market leader for using alternative therapy to stay fit or recover from injury.

'He was always seeking alternative medicines and going to different health practitioners that we all thought at the time were witch doctors,' says Lyon.

On one occasion Lyon walked into the physio room to check in on Stynes, who had suffered an ankle injury in training. A horrible smell filled his nose as he entered. Stynes was sitting on the edge of the physio table rubbing a smoking 'cigar-type thing' over his ankle. The physios were fuming that Stynes was making a mockery of their jobs, but he didn't care.

'He played 244 games in a row, which will never, ever be beaten. When you look back on it you have to say that Jim was right and the rest of the footy world was wrong.

'AFL football was going through this big transition where we'd gone from part-time to full-time. Our era was sort of caught right in the middle.

'Football had always been played in a manner — everyone trained the same way and recovered the same way. And Jim would never accept that. He would say, 'Okay that's the way it was done, but there might be a better way to do it.'

* * *

CROKE PARK, 2002

Lyon was two years retired when he was appointed Australia's International Rules coach in 2001. It was a surprise to no-one that Stynes was Lyon's right-hand man and assistant coach for the four years he led Australia.

'When they asked I jumped at it and I loved every minute,' he says.

'I had an added incentive with my history, with the whole Ireland-Australia thing with Jim and the Melbourne footy club who have been pioneers to a large degree in trying to bring players over.

'Jimmy was my best mate so to have him sitting alongside me in the coaches' box was great. Travelling back to Ireland with him and getting a sense of Ireland through his eyes was really special. I look back on those times now he's not with us anymore, they were some of my favourites times of my life .

'All of those things combined made the whole experience really memorable for me. I just love the way the Irish go about things as well. They've got a great perspective and outlook.

'I enjoyed the company of the Irish people I met, I loved seeing the players going about it, I loved talking to the press when I was over there. I just think it was one of the best things I've done.'

Led by Lyon and Stynes, Australia won two series and lost two between 2001 and 2004. As a recently retired player, the manager was conscious that the series took place during the AFL off-season, so he wasn't a total disciplinarian.

'While I wanted to make sure we respected the occasion and were professional about it, it was always at the end of our football season,' Lyon says. 'So I was trusting of the group and said, 'Listen, you've the opportunity to go out, have a beer and that sort of stuff but two or three nights before, let's pull-up, let's do what we need to do and make the night of the game even bigger.'

'It was great craic,' he laughs. 'That was a word that we came to know. We had the great Robert DiPierdomenico, the Dipper, and he was our social organiser. He did a great job.'

There were fun times, but they had some very serious moments too. Not least prior to the first Test of that tour in 2002. The night before, the Australian camp received news of the horrific terrorist attacks on the Indonesian island of Bali that became known as the Bali Bombings.

AFL players often holiday in Bali during the off-season, and many members of the Australian squad in Dublin had teammates on the island.

Three bombs were detonated, killing 88 Australians and 204 people in total. Osama bin Laden later claimed responsibility for the bombings, saying it was a retaliation for Australia's support of the United States' war on terror.

'We had a meeting the night before the first Test and a couple of players were running late. I started to get a bit angry about it,' says Lyon. 'Then we realised this bomb had gone off in Bali and the team-mates of a lot of the players were on holidays in Bali.

'These players were in their rooms, trying to find information about whether or not their team-mates were still alive. We all went to bed that night, we understood how big a thing it was, but we didn't know if some of the team-mates of the players were dead or alive.

'We made the point that the next day when we played, that we would be the first Australian team, the first sporting team to represent the country since this tragic event and how important it was that we put our best foot forward.'

Mark Bickley was part of the Aussie squad that year and he recently appeared on SEN Breakfast, an entertaining Melbourne sports radio show co-presented by Lyon.

'One of the only photos I've got up in my house is us standing arm-in-arm under the Aussie flag at half-mast, observing a minute's silence,' Bickley told his former manager.

'You can see the emotion on everyone's face and it's pretty spectacular. At that stage there was still some people missing and we all presumed the worst.

'Being away from home, with the minute's silence and the

national anthem, it was one of the most emotional times I've ever been on a sporting field.

'Without blowing up your tyres too much Garry, your pre-match speech about us having the first chance for an Aussie team to represent our country and show them what we were made of — I thought that was very special.'

Lyon says he didn't prepare the famous speech, but instead 'gauged the mood of the group' and rolled with it.

'If any player came up and said I can't play because of the circumstances then absolutely you'd have understood but no-one did. We were all in it together. As always when you travel to Ireland there was the us against them mentality. Seventy-odd thousand at Croke Park is a pretty intimidating venue and I think the players all found some strength in support from each other.

'I never really pre-planned anything when I spoke. Those were unprecedented circumstances. We tried to get that sense of your country and representing everyone anyway, but on that particular occasion it was even more profound.

'Mark said it was a memory he'll never forget and I won't either,' he adds.

* * *

MELBOURNE, 2012

Near the end of Stynes' battle with cancer, Lyon was constantly by his side.

'In the last months of Jim's life, I spent a lot of time just sitting with him in hospital or at home,' he says. 'We just had that time to talk which men don't normally have.

'We had hours and hours of philosophical discussion about

different things and it became really obvious how different the two of us were. And how I think most people when they measured themselves against Jim would feel inadequate.

'He wasn't meaning to do it to me but he had a much broader understanding of life at that early stage of his life. I learned a lot. His sense of country I spoke about, his love of Ireland and his sense of their history, which I didn't have the same of my country. Then his relationships with his family and his vulnerabilities, all the things which we should be but we aren't always. He was a pillar, he stood out in that area.'

Stynes wrote in his book: 'We talked for hours. We spoke about trivial stuff, like the merit of wine gums versus jubes. We reminisced, and reassured each other that we really were pretty decent footballers in our day.

'Like a few of my closer mates, Garry and I had found it easier to open up in recent months. We could talk about our emotions, our fears, our insecurities and our passions.'

Lyon tells a great story of the time Stynes' wife Sam left the former team-mates alone in the hospital while she went home to check on the kids. She gave Lyon strict instructions that her husband was to take it easy.

In the meantime, Stynes wanted to stretch his legs, so the pair went for a stroll around the ward at 2am. Along the way, they happened to stumble across a mini pool table.

Some time later, Sam returned to an empty hospital bed. She heard some shouting coming from down the corridor and walked down to find the pair having a heated argument beside the pool table.

They were arguing over whether you could shoot backwards after receiving two free shots, and neither man was giving an inch.

Stynes had come out of brain surgery just 24 hours earlier, was connected to an IV machine and had failing eyesight, but he had lost none of his competitiveness.

During those lengthy discussions in the final months, Lyon says they got to know each other on a whole new level. That's remarkable, considering the pair were friends for 27 years by that point.

'It was the most special time,' he says. 'You don't realise until you go through it and have those conversations, it's a bit of a journey and you learn about yourself in the process.

'I refer back to him, you end up measuring yourself by him and who he was in terms of the way you live your life. I find myself often thinking, 'What would Jim think about that?' That is a pretty special thing.'

And who won that game of pool in the hospital?

'He beat me.'

TWELVE

NET LOSS AS SCOTT EVANS HANGS UP HIS BADMINTON RACKET

—

STEVE O'ROURKE | 7 FEBRUARY

ON TUESDAY MORNING, Scott Evans was doing something he's done nearly every day since he was a young child. He was playing badminton. In between practice sessions, Evans walked over to his phone and spotted there were dozens upon dozens of notifications. 'They know now,' he thought to himself as he put the phone back down.

But as he wiped his brow and walked over to the same court he has played on thousands of times before, something felt different. He had a spring in his step he hadn't felt for some time. Almost as if an enormous weight had been lifted off his shoulders.

Atlas shrugged indeed.

'Do you know when you take a big deep breath and it releases all the tension from your body?' Evans asked *The42* yesterday.

'I'm not joking, when I went back out onto that court I felt about 10kg lighter than I've done in months. I just feel like it will be healthy for me to step away from the pressure of the past 14 years, the pressure I put myself under more than most.'

Since the age of 16, probably even before, badminton has been Evans's life. He gave up school in Dublin for the sport he loves, moving to Denmark when he was still a child to train full-time. He has sacrificed time with friends for hours getting fitter and stronger in the gym. He has celebrated family birthdays over Skype because he was off playing tournaments in Lithuania or Brazil.

But more than that, Evans has taken it on himself to play the role of badminton evangelist, trying to convince fans, the media and even some governing bodies that the sport he has played since the age of five was worth attending, worth covering, worth funding.

Even now, just a day or so removed from officially announcing his retirement, he remains unequivocal about his love of badminton and what he can do to promote it. However, he's also realistic that the sport, and those taking part in it, can always do more to make it mainstream.

'ONE THING I do wonder about is, if I'd been based in Dublin when I was going to three Olympics and on the verge of the world's top-20, would there have been more media coverage of badminton outside of the Olympic cycle? But, then I tell myself that, if I was based in Dublin, I'd never have reached the level I reached because I wouldn't be training with some of the best players in the world on a daily basis.

'I chose to put my career first, to get as much out of that as I could over building the profile of badminton in Ireland. A lot of people I've talked to in the media, they all understand why I've done that, but they also all say they'd have been able to do so much more around the sport if I was back in Dublin.'

In 2011, Evans found himself in trouble both on and off the court. At the Norwegian International he was serving to stay in his quarter-final against Yuhan Tan of Belgium and felt that an umpire had incorrectly called his serve on match point out, giving Tan the game.

It was far from the first questionable decision that went against Evans that afternoon and, combined with the fact it was not the first time he had come up against the official in question, he lashed out, shouting expletives before walking off the court without shaking hands with the umpire.

'It's been quite hard for me at times, I've really struggled,' he says.

'Back in 2011, when I got that black card for misbehaving on court, I knew there was something really wrong.

'To put it in perspective, there have only ever been four black cards issued in the history of badminton and, at the very least, a black card means you get disqualified from the tournament straight away. Depending on the circumstances of the card, you can be banned for six months or even banned for life. My situation wasn't really as bad as the others, so I just took a heavy fine and I could play again the following week.

'But at that time, I was in the worst place I've ever been. I was only sleeping an hour a night. I couldn't eat. I was just in a terrible place. A couple of times throughout my career — sometimes down to injury, sometimes down to bad results — I've really, really struggled.

'When the news of my retirement came out yesterday, it just felt like the pressure I've been carrying around with me for so many years, it's now off my shoulders. Jesus, I'm just so glad it's over because I don't need to worry about it anymore, I don't need to put myself under all that pressure.

'Thinking back on what life was like following the black card though. I mean, fuck, I was in a dark place. I don't know if it was depression, but I know it was a really difficult time for me and I know how much I struggled. From reading other stories from other people who've struggled with depression, I don't doubt now that it was. But I think the period since has defined the person I am now. I went through the first couple of months literally on my own on a daily basis and I knew that something had to happen for my attitude and my life to change and I thought that I was the only person who could change it,' he says.

2011 wasn't the first time Evans had doubts about his place in the world though. When he first moved to Denmark he could so easily have jumped on an aeroplane and returned to the safety of home. It was all a long way from the joy he felt when he first picked up a racket.

'I think the actual reason I first had a badminton racket in my hand was more to use as a weapon than anything else,' he jokes. 'I remember just going around and smashing the shit out of things in my house, chasing my brother — Lee — with it trying to smash him.

'But seriously, my mum and dad have obviously been involved in the game for ages. My dad has two sport shops which are racket-based — tennis, squash, badminton — so there's always been a connection to badminton in my family.

'Lee, he's two years older than me and he'd already started playing badminton at that stage, so I'd be down in the hall when he was going down to play or I'd be in my dad's shop and we'd always take rackets and play on a makeshift court. There's always been that connection and, I guess, it always seems to work out that way with kids; they always get into whatever their parents are involved in and that's the same thing that happened for me.'

A prodigious talent, Evans often beat boys much older than him in the underage ranks. But while his ability and love of the sport grew, so too did his frustrations with its set up in Ireland. That didn't stop him training twice a day most days, mind.

The absence of any sort of path to becoming a professional would prove too much. Bored in school, bored with the lack of real competition, Copenhagen came calling. Looking back with adult eyes, it feels like an incredibly ballsy move. But Evans was still a child. In his own mind he was invincible, he was infallible, it was absolutely the right thing to do.

Until he got there.

'I remember the first week I moved to Denmark. It was January and it was fucking freezing. There was just snow everywhere and it was pitch black in the morning, only getting bright at 10am and it was dark again at 4pm

'I was in a house with four other players, going to practice twice a day and, because I was practising full-time, I'd no energy to do anything else. My first eight months over there was basically get up, eat breakfast, go to training, come back, eat lunch, sleep a bit, wake up, eat, go back to practice, come home, have dinner and go back to bed again. That was it, every day for eight months.

'And it didn't start off great for me either. Literally the first week I moved there, I got a huge shock with the weather but I'd also eaten something bad so I had food poisoning for the first four days. I was incredibly ill with that and, to top it all off, I was missing my dad's 50th birthday party. As I was lying in bed in an absolute heap, he rang me when my family were all together for his birthday and he put the phone on loudspeaker and I remember chatting to everyone back home thinking 'What have I gotten myself into?' I was stuck in a bed, in a foreign country, I don't know the language, I'm in a heap puking, just wondering what the hell was going on?

'It was a shock, but I wanted to play full-time so much, I stuck at it. Now I'll never, ever tell anyone it was easy, because it was tough for me. There were plenty of times during the first eight months that I had doubts that it really was for me. A couple of the Irish players have tried to do this and they've realised it isn't for them and they've moved home again. So it's certainly not for everyone but I just kept at it, kept digging away.'

The effort would eventually pay off.

In 2008 Evans qualified for the Beijing Olympic Games, becoming the first Irish man to represent his country in the sport of badminton. For a man so proud of his nation, who loves few things more than pulling on an Irish shirt to play as the tricolour waves courtside, it was a moment that you would think would mean a lot personally.

But, once more, it was the sport of badminton that was front and centre for Evans.

'To be honest, I've never once thought that, because I was the first male to play badminton for Ireland at an Olympic Games, that it was — in and of itself — an achievement. I don't know, for me, for my career, it was just part of the overall journey. But I never thought of it as making history or anything like that, I only thought of it as something that would help the sport of badminton in Ireland by giving it some more publicity.

'But it's funny how these things turn out. I got to the Olympics in Beijing and I lost to Marc Zwiebler in a very close match that could have gone either way. Eight years later and I end up playing Marc again in Rio, only this time, it goes my way and I'd go on to have a very good Games.

'That result in Beijing though, I can't tell you how much that hurt me for so many years. Even just playing Marc. Every time I met him in a tournament after 2008, the Beijing feeling I had after I lost to him came back to me and I always found it very difficult to beat him. I just couldn't get over it.'

2012 brought another Olympics and another first round loss, this time to China's Lin Dan, the world number one. There was no shame in a loss to a player of that calibre, but after his personal struggles in 2011, it just felt like the sport might be getting away from Evans a little bit. Was he wrong to have invested so much time, poured so much of his heart into a sport when it must have felt he was getting so little in return?

The night, as they say, is darkest just before the dawn and 2012 would end for Evans with — until Rio 2016 — the biggest moment of his career, victory at the Irish Open.

'I can't explain the feelings that I had the moment I won that tournament. I literally don't have the words. The amount of joy I felt in my body and my mind was out of this world. It was really a huge thing for me.

'The first time I went out to watch the Irish Open as a little kid, I was probably about six or seven at the time. I went with my dad and it took place in the same hall as where I ended up winning the tournament. I remember saying to my brother a couple of times that, if I only ever won one tournament in my entire career, I would like it to be the Irish Open.

'When you've been thinking about something your whole career, with the pressure you put yourself under being Irish and with the pressure that came with being the number one seed, to go on and win it that week was amazing. I couldn't hold it together afterwards either. If you go onto YouTube there's an interview where I just can't talk after the win because I was so emotional about the whole thing but I'm still handed this fucking microphone to give my reaction and I couldn't get a word out of my mouth,' he laughs.

But what had changed for Evans, what had helped him over the line to win a tournament he'd focused on winning his entire playing career? As you may have guessed by now, a large part of it was his own drive and determination, but he had some help from an unexpected source: Keith Barry.

Yes, that Keith Barry: self-described magician, hypnotist and mentalist, among other things.

'After what happened in 2011, I had to find out not just who I was as a person, but who I wanted to be. People in the badminton world saw me as a certain person, they knew my attitude, they knew my personality and I needed to change that in a lot of ways.

'For the first couple of months, I took that challenge on myself and something that I learned a lot over the years — I've worked with a lot of sports psychologists — is that, at the end of the day, the best way for me was figuring it out for myself. That's what worked best for me. During that time, every minute that I was awake I spent trying to figure out who I am, who I wanted to be and that period has absolutely led on to the person I am now and the results that I've achieved since, there's no doubt about it.'

He adds: 'It was just a matter of finding someone who, in a way, fits with your personality and for me, working with Keith I finally felt that his way of doing it was perfect and he was absolutely the right person to help me through a tough situation, through a very rough fucking period. Not only that, he helped me get to the next level in my career. To this day I still use the techniques he gave me and the things we talked about to help me and I'm so grateful for what he did for me. I have a lot of time for him and a lot of things to thank him for.'

What followed was the most successful spell of the Dubliner's career. He won the 2013 Cyprus International, the 2014 Brazil Open and, by 2015, achieved a world ranking of 23. All that was left was to get to Rio to secure a first win at the Olympic Games.

When the draw came out, the badminton gods had conspired to ensure that Marc Zwiebler, his nemesis from 2008 and in almost every match they had played since, would be in his group. And fate would dictate that he would play the German first.

History, world ranking and pretty quickly the score were on Zwiebler's side as he raced into a one-set lead, 21-9.

But Evans dug deep and, playing like a man possessed, took the second set 21-17. Even when he was 5-1 down in the third, Evans refused to give up and won 20 of the next 22 points to take the final set 21-7 to become the first Irishman to win a badminton match at the Olympic Games.

'People probably don't realise just how much the result in Rio meant to me,' he says.

'They'll look at it and say 'Yeah, great win' but it meant so much more than just a first win at an Olympic Games. I'm convinced that all these things happen for a reason. I can't help but feel it was on purpose that I was put into a group with Marc at Rio, it was just meant to be that I'd meet him and go on to finally win at what turned out to be my last Olympics.'

It wasn't supposed to be his last, of course. Aged 30, Evans had hoped to qualify for Tokyo 2020 and while his announcement yesterday may have come as a surprise to many in Irish sport, he actually took the decision well before Christmas.

The period between deciding to retire and announcing it officially has given Evans an opportunity to reflect on everything, from beating the shite out of his brother with a racket at the age of five to dominating a home-court favourite in Ygor Coelho de Oliveira to qualify for the knockout stages of the 2016 Olympics.

But, as he has done his whole career, he's found himself thinking about the state he's left the sport of badminton in as much as his own achievements.

'I've had an incredible career, especially when you consider the circumstances and the position I was in when I started out on this journey. To achieve what I've achieved feels incredible and I never really had a chance to reflect on that during my career — I don't think people playing top-level sport ever really do — but now that I've decided I'm stopping, I can't help but think back on it all.

'But what I am really proud of is the systems in place for badminton in Ireland now. It's still not perfect at the moment for some players, but things are being put in place and that's the most important thing. You can't move forward without putting systems in place and, to be fair to Badminton Ireland, they're doing that and I've no doubt over the next couple of years there'll be more players coming into the system and getting better and better results because of that.

'And I do feel like I've played a big part in that. A lot of messages I've received since the announcement was made public show that other people think I've played a big part in that. That's something I've very, very proud of.

'I'll always have a big heart for badminton, especially in Ireland and — like I said to Badminton Ireland and the Sports

Council when I informed them I was retiring — if there's ever anything I can do, in any way at all, to help them or to support badminton in Ireland, then I'm only a phone call away.'

Atlas may have shrugged, but you can't help but feel his respite was only temporary.

THIRTEEN

THE LIMERICK LAD WHO MARKED MARADONA AND BATTLED REAL MADRID IN THE EUROPEAN CUP

—

AARON GALLAGHER | 5 AUGUST

DESPITE A CAREER which saw him battle against Vicente del Bosque in front of 60,000 spectators at the Bernabéu, mark a 19-year-old prodigy named Diego Maradona in Buenos Aires and win the league and FAI Cup alongside his boyhood heroes, there is only one achievement Pat Nolan is willing to boast about.

'I worked with John Player for nearly 30 years, and I never smoked a cigarette in my life,' he jests. 'I never touched one and never had the inclination to.'

The former Limerick defender has a lot of stories to tell — drinking quiet pints with Ray Wilkins, playing golf with Bryan Robson, swapping shirts with Kevin Keegan, being battered up and down the pitch by Brazil at the Estádio Rei Pelé a year before they lit up the 1982 World Cup.

But he's been reluctant to tell them since he retired and that hesitancy to speak about his experiences is perhaps the reason why his name does not fall off the tongue like other League of Ireland greats, whose stories we could each reel off at the drop of a hat.

He puts it down to embarrassment, and says that his career as an 'average player' is nothing to boast about. But the right word is modesty, and the self-deprecation of a footballer who was a core part of Limerick's greatest ever generation (capped at Under-21 level for Ireland and named in the 1980 Soccer Writers' Team of the Year), as well as a player who shared the field of play with some of football's most iconic stars.

Joining Limerick in 1974 as an 18-year-old from local side Wembley Rovers, there was no reason to believe an extraordinary career which would see him play games in places like the San Mamés and River Plate lay ahead.

In fact, until his mid-teens, the Henry Street boy hardly even touched the ball with his feet.

'Up to the age of about 15 I actually played in goal,' he laughs. 'The team was so good and no-one wanted to play there, so I got stuck between the sticks for a few years... call me a late developer.'

Growing up in Limerick in the late 1950s was not glamorous, he admits. He namechecks Angela's Ashes and contrasts Frank McCourt's portrayal to his own youth on Knockdown's Lane.

Today the average attendance at the Markets Field is a little over 1,000 for home games. With Limerick preparing for an All-Ireland hurling final and the popularity and success at Thomond Park, it's easy to think football was always a secondary or tertiary choice as a spectator sport.

But that couldn't be further from the truth, Nolan attests. Limerick is, was and always will be enchanted with football, as was his own experience.

'In '65 and '66 Limerick were beaten in two FAI Cup finals

back-to-back by Shamrock Rovers — that would have had a huge influence on me, as well as the team in 1971 who managed to get over the line.

'I got off school to see that game. They beat Drogheda on a miserable Wednesday 3-0 in the cup replay — it was a great night for Limerick because it was the first time in the club's history to actually win the FAI Cup.

'The year we won the league we were getting 7,000 or 8,000 people at the Markets Field every fortnight, it was just jammers. But then again, there was nothing for people in those days.'

The arrival of Eoin Hand, who would later manage Ireland for five years, completely transformed the fortunes of football in Limerick in 1979.

Coming to the end of his own playing career, a 33-year-old Hand swapped Portsmouth for the League of Ireland in a move which would alter the course of history for the Blues, ushering the team into what is still proclaimed to be a golden generation it has never come close to matching, or surpassing.

A league title — the club's first in 20 years — a league cup, an FAI Cup and three consecutive years of football against European opponents like Real Madrid, Southampton and AZ Alkmaar saw a new era of untold success sweep through the crumbling fortress that was the Markets Field in Garryowen.

Before Eoin Hand, Limerick were much as they are now, Nolan attests — struggling, punching low at the bottom of the table, flirting with the threat of relegation. But after his arrival, the side grew in stature, he says, commanded a new bullishness and built on the momentum of a new structure of professionalism which their new manager enforced from the get-go.

LIMERICK'S OWN LEAGUE title under Hand in 1979-80 was an incredible feat but the manner in which it was earned, by taking a team bottom of the table just a handful of seasons earlier, adds more weight and veneer to the success. Pat Nolan admits winning leagues was something which seemed a world away from Limerick's ambitions when he made his debut as an 18-year-old.

But Hand changed everything, arriving off the boat from England to take his first managerial role. Player-manager, as it were, with the bossman chipping in with more than a handful of goals which helped steer his side up the table, on one occasion scoring all four in a 4-0 win over Cork United.

Hand even brought his own lawnmower to cut the desperately poor playing surface at the Markets Field and that fact alone offers an insight into the desire he had for Limerick to fulfil its true potential, to stand tall alongside teams like Shamrock Rovers, Dundalk and Athlone.

'Ah, he changed everything. Absolutely everything,' Nolan reflects.

'It was a combination of Eoin and a lot of credit has to go to the fitness coach David Mahedy, because back in '80 the key reason we won the league was due to the fact that we were so fit and agile.

'We trained really hard, we really did train like full-time pros. I remember Eoin brought us over to Portsmouth mid-season one time. We were after getting beaten by Bohemians in Dalymount and the following Monday we were taken away for a week to recharge the batteries.

'Portsmouth were away at the time and Eoin took us to Fratton Park where he told one of the fitness coaches: 'Listen I want you to really hammer these guys.' The man did everything in his power and by the end of the week he said, 'Eoin, these lads are as fit as any team in England.' I think that worked.

'Both David and Eoin were fantastic. He was the boss in one sense and he was one of the boys too. He could mix it, he could have his few pints with us, but you knew when to draw the line. It was very much a case of, 'Don't step over this line, I'm the boss' — and he let you know fairly quickly.

'He was brilliant, just brilliant. I'll tell you a story, actually,' Nolan grins.

'I remember we went to Ballybofey to play Finn Harps on a Saturday, and we stayed overnight where we always did in Brian McEniff's hotel, the Holyrood in Bundoran.

'We played the game, it was probably the match that won us the league in 1980 — 2-0 down with 15 minutes to go, we score in the last minute to beat them 3-2. We arrived back in the hotel and Eoin says, 'Right lads, drinks are on me.'

'On the Wednesday I was getting married. But anyway, we went back to the hotel, had our meal, had a few pints until the bar closed, which was 11 or 12 at night. We're still four-and-a-half hours from getting back to Limerick and down the stairs we go to a disco.

'We arrived back in Limerick at 10am, and they were all due to go to my stag that night... they never showed up. None of them — they were all plastered. Tony Morris went into work, he was in the Krups factory at the time. He went to work, went into the loo, fell asleep and the boys woke him at 4.30pm and told him to go home: 'Your shift is over, Tony.'

'No, but in all fairness Eoin was very good,' Nolan adds. 'Man-management-wise, there was no one better. He knew how to deal with players. Different people need different ways to get them going and motivate them, and he was very good at that. I thought he was very unlucky as the Irish manager... one goal [against Belgium] and he would have been the hero instead of Jack Charlton.'

Hand succeeded in leading Limerick to its first League of Ireland title since 1960, claiming the silverware thanks to that dramatic 3-2 victory away to Finn Harps before a tense and fraught 1-1 draw against third-placed Athlone sealed it. An infamous match which lives long in the memory of all supporters.

The visitors brought thousands of fans draped in blue with them to Athlone to witness their crowning moment, but an error from goalkeeper Kevin Fitzpatrick, where he bizarrely picked the ball up outside his own box, allowed the hosts to sweep in a stunning free-kick to snatch the lead.

'We were nervous — the league was on the line for us. One game, we needed a draw. And we were nervous. I reckon there were 7,000 people from Limerick packed in there like sardines.

'Actually, it was probably even more than that. I'd say 15,000 people would tell you they were in St Mel's Park that day. It was a bit like the All Blacks game against Munster — everyone will tell you they were at it.'

A penalty from Tony Meaney levelled proceedings, Limerick held on for dear life, and a point was enough to secure a first title in two decades.

Did he think Limerick would still be waiting for their next league title 28 years later?

'Not on your life,' Nolan says. 'We were looking at it the following year thinking, 'We'll do it again,' and we came very close. You did think the good times were going to last forever, absolutely. We had the chance to do the double that year in 1980, and we were done by Waterford in a semi-final replay in Milltown. It really was a golden era for football in Limerick at that time and you did think it was going to last forever.'

Winning the league in 1980 meant the prospect of European football. But there's a big difference between a game on the continent and being drawn to play Real Madrid in the opening round of the European Cup — let alone in a season where the Spanish giants would make it all the way to the final, where they were undone by an Alan Kennedy strike for Liverpool in Rome.

'We thought it was a joke,' Nolan exhales remembering the moment he and his team-mates found out that they would be playing the La Liga champions at home and then away at the Santiago Bernabéu.

'It was like somebody was having us on when we heard. It couldn't be, it was just unbelievable. But to be honest with you, even though they had won the European Cup how many, six times, Eoin Hand made us believe that they were only 11 men, just like us. And looking back... I still think it was a game we should have won,' he says.

'It's one of the few regrets that I have, the fact that we should have beaten them. I'm not being smart or clever by saying that, but we should have. We were the better team on the day. We were 1-0 up and Johnny Matthews had a goal disallowed which was proven afterwards wasn't actually offside.

'That goal would have seen us go 2-0 up. We were one up with 15 minutes to go and Fitzpatrick got a rush of blood to the head and gave away a penalty.'

The game was moved to Lansdowne Road due to the poor condition of the Markets Field. But just 7,000 supporters turned out in Dublin for the glamour fixture, with the decision to move the game away from Limerick a point of contention which still does not sit well with supporters and players alike almost three decades on.

Despite Des Kennedy putting the League of Ireland side ahead with a deft finish, a Juanito penalty was followed by a second-half winner from Pineda, who poked in a free-kick to snatch a 2-1 win for Madrid.

'We had played very well all night and we were not in any way overawed by them,' says Nolan on the first leg in Dublin. 'They certainly did not put us on the rack at any stage. When we got in at half-time we were saying to ourselves, 'Lads, this crowd are there for the taking.'

'Had they not got the penalty, which was nothing more than bad judgement on Alan's part, I don't think they would have ever scored. I think we would have won 1-0. The penalty gave us away and deflated us a small bit. We switched off for another free-kick, they scored from it and that was that.'

The second leg, Nolan says, was simply the stuff of fairytales. The legendary Santiago Bernabéu, over 60,000 supporters packing the stands, stacked high in endless, tall rows one on top of another and little old Limerick standing opposed to 11 men draped in those iconic white shirts.

The right back was just 23 years old stepping out into this cauldron at the heart of the Spanish capital. Nolan wasn't overly taken aback by the size of the occasion.

This was a football match, he says today, 28 years on. A game of football he desperately, desperately wanted to win. Limerick had not been taken for mugs in the opening leg, had led Real Madrid 1-0 and could still do the unimaginable and dump the six-time European champions out on their own patch.

There wasn't time to be nervous and there wasn't a need to be overawed, even facing off against players like Spain's

World Cup-winning manager Vincent del Bosque. Much like their days of battling the top sides in the League of Ireland in the mid-1970s, Limerick had nothing to lose and everything to gain.

'Were we intimidated? No, to be honest,' he says. 'You kind of blank everything out and I personally never had any issues on the pitch. You blank the crowd out no matter what the size, and as you get older you start to hear any bad things that they are shouting at you.

'But when you're younger, you're fearless and you're involved in the game and it doesn't faze you one bit. We went into the stadium the day before and they wouldn't let us walk out onto the pitch unless we took off our shoes.

'That is a fact, that is gospel. At that stage the ground was a bit dilapidated and it needed a bit of renovation and modernisation. But all that said, how many people can say they played in the Bernabéu?'

Despite their confidence and desire to cause one of the biggest upsets in European history, things didn't go to plan. Des Kennedy replicated his achievement at Lansdowne Road and scored at the Bernabéu, but five goals past Kevin Fitzpatrick saw the night end in a 5-1 loss in Madrid and a humbling 7-2 aggregate defeat.

'It probably wasn't a fair reflection of the effort that we put into it,' Nolan says. 'Going into the game with a scoreline of 7-2 against a team like Real Madrid, you'd nearly expect that. It was always going to get away from us in the away leg though, they were always going to put us under pressure — and they did.'

After the low of Madrid, success continued for Limerick two years later, winning the FAI Cup in 1982 for the first time in

11 years. Like their league title success leading to a European fixture with Madrid, their third-placed finish in 1981 brought with it another glamour tie — facing Southampton in the Uefa Cup opening round, a game which ended in a 3-0 defeat at home, but saw a famous 1-1 draw at The Dell.

'We played them here in the Uefa Cup. Going off at half-time I said to Kevin Keegan, 'Mr Keegan' — I didn't dare to call him Kevin — 'Mr Keegan', I said, 'Any chance of getting your jersey?' I told him I had a testimonial coming up and that I was going to raffle it off.

"Sorry,' he said, 'I promised it to someone here already, but when you come over to England for the second leg I'll look after you.'

'I said to myself, 'Well Pat, there's no chance of that happening, he'll forget it by that stage.'

'So we went over anyway — now remember, swapping jerseys in those days wasn't the done thing and it was only slowly coming into fashion — but Lawrie McMenemy came into our dressing room with a BBC crew because they were doing some sort of a documentary on Tony Ward.

'There was pandemonium in the dressing room, we had gotten a great result drawing with Southampton 1-1. You were looking at guys like Alan Ball, Mick Channon, Mark Wright, Kevin Keegan, Ivan Golac, Steve Moran — they had some team.

'But anyway, the manager McMenemy came in and said, 'Lads, just as a mark of respect for your performance, you can swap shirts with our lads.'

'My team-mate Brendan Storan was off like a shot down into the home dressing room in search of Keegan. He walked up to him and said, 'Kevin, any chance of your jersey?'

'Keegan looked at Brendan and said: 'I'm sorry, I promised it to the full-back in Limerick.' And that's a true story — he remembered what I had said to him at the Markets Field and he had kept the jersey for me,' says Nolan.

'I just thought, 'What a man' — he was true to his word. What a man. I would put him in the same ilk as Robson and Wilkins — they were just gentlemen. Gentlemen. Because don't forget, he was a superstar at that time after being European Player of the Year and winning the Ballon d'Or playing at Hamburg and Liverpool. He was just a gent, a gent.'

Nolan mentions Wilkins and Robson, and naturally there's a story in there too. After almost a decade of service to Limerick, he was given a glamour testimonial against Manchester United at the Markets Field in 1982.

Ron Atkinson arrived in Garryowen alongside stars like Kevin Moran, Gordon McQueen, Garry Birtles and Frank Stapleton for a one-off match in recognition of the defender's loyalty and achievements in the blue shirt of Limerick.

'It was a great night. I was fortunate — they were over to play in Don Gibbons' testimonial in Dublin. I think Eoin was reasonably friendly with Atkinson and he got Man United to bring them down. It wasn't cheap either, I think it cost about £15,000 back then.

'It was a great occasion and they were a great bunch of fellas. I spent the night with Bryan Robson and Ray Wilkins.

'Wilkins was just a gentleman down to his shoes,' he says very seriously.

'That lad… he just oozes class. I was so sorry to hear when he passed away. I brought him out to one of the local golf clubs the day before the match. I play golf up there and was a member and I asked the club would they let them play, and it was no problem organising clubs and everything for them.

'I think most of them were playing golf themselves at that stage. They were all in their tracksuits and whatever else, but Wilkins didn't play golf and he came in for the presentation dressed in his official Man United club suit, shirt and tie.

'Real quality now. He stood up and thanked the golf club for having them, thanked all the staff, signed autographs for everyone, just an unbelievable man. Later that night I had a few pints with them. Robson and himself were just so down to earth, two of the nicest guys I ever met.'

You can hear in his voice the reverence that Nolan has for all that he achieved with Limerick. Not personal achievement, but the fact that it came with his local club, the club he supported on Sunday afternoons when there was nothing else for a kid on Henry Street to do.

Climbing out from the stand and onto the pitch to share titles and cups with his boyhood heroes are his favourites memories. But outside of his club career came some fascinating trips abroad, which he admits again he was fortunate to experience.

A trip to Buenos Aires in 1982 saw a League of Ireland XI face world champions Argentina at the River Plate stadium. Nolan had the task of picking up a tricky forward by the name of Diego Maradona but, like so many others, he couldn't keep him scoreless — the magnetic 19-year-old rifling a stunning left-footed effort into the top corner to snatch a 1-0 win.

'It was a backs-to-the-wall performance, but we got an unbelievable result all things considered. They went to Dublin the following week and beat the Republic 1-0 in Lansdowne. Maradona was just exceptional, even then you could see it.

'I picked him up, I had the job of marking him. The lads

will testify on my behalf, I don't think I kicked the ball all night,' he laughs. 'I don't think I kicked the ball and I didn't kick him either — you couldn't get near him he was that good. I couldn't get close.

'I asked him for his jersey and he wouldn't give it to me, which is the one disappointing thing from the night in Argentina. Now I can speak a small bit of Spanish and I'm convinced if I had the language back then maybe there was a chance he would have given it to me. Maybe he would have been a bit more giving.

'But even at that stage — I think he was only 18 or 19 — he was a kid thinking, 'Who's this Irish fella?' which was fair enough. I somehow managed to get myself into a great photograph of him actually scoring the goal. Some Spanish magazine snapped it and it ended up on the cover — Paddy Duggan to the side, me sliding in to try and get a block in, and the man himself Maradona taking a shot which flew into the top corner.

'I got there as quick as I could but it wasn't enough,' Nolan says heartily. 'It was some goal, too, I think it was Alan Patterson in goal for us that night. I don't think Alan saw too much of it, the shot flew past him in the blink of an eye. An almighty strike, it was just incredible.

'He was quick, Maradona... and let me tell you, he was built solid. He was a little shit to play against but in the best possible way. A serious competitor and all the talent in the world. They didn't score in the second half... so we must have done something right.'

If the Argentina game was a tight contest with a 1-0 defeat, a meeting with Brazil at the brand new Estádio Rei Pelé in September 1982 did not yield anywhere near as close a game, with the League of Ireland XI being pummelled 6-0.

'Brazil were probably the best side I've ever seen and they probably should have won the World Cup in 1982. We played against 10 of their regulars… Socrates was the only one missing. We flew into Rio and had another two and a half hour flight to get to Maceió. They hadn't had an international game there in 25 years and this match with us was in the new Pele Stadium — it was just full to capacity, 55,000.

'The game was on at 9pm and it was packed at 6pm. There was at least another 10,000 outside. It was unbelievable, it really was. They beat us 6-0, Zico scored four. I think Tony McConville got his jersey and I got Éder's. I gave all of my jerseys away and it's the only one I've kept.

'It was amazing then to see the same lads we played against rock up at the 1982 World Cup the following year, Paolo Rossi scoring a hat-trick to beat them in the second round. They say it was the best Brazil team since 1970 and one of the best, along with the Dutch in '74, never to win the World Cup.'

Three years before that, Nolan featured against the Basque national team, in what was the nation's first football match since 1937 as the dictatorial Franco regime clamped down on the game throughout the following decades.

Xabi Alonso's father, Miguel Ángel Alonso, was just one name on the opposition team-sheet. The match was organised to round off the annual Aste Nagusia (Basque week of celebration), with 45,000 frenzied supporters packing Athletic Bilbao's San Mamés for the occasion — a 4-1 win for the hosts.

'They hadn't played since 1937 as a country and you know the Basques… they want their independence, just like the Catalans. I didn't realise the significance of the game until years afterwards when I read up about it.

'Again like a lot of these games, it was just a fantastic

occasion and we were privileged to be a part of it. Ronnie Whelan played for us and he scored a goal on the night... they beat us 4-1. We played very, very well and oddly enough played in an all-blue strip with an Irish crest.'

We've been speaking for well over an hour and despite spending much of that time laying praise at the feet of his team-mates, Nolan fails to mention one game in particular.

Suddenly his modesty becomes all the more transparent, as he needs to be chided into talking about the goal he scored against AZ Alkmaar in the European Cup Winners' Cup in 1982.

'I remember it very clearly,' he says after a while. 'Eoin [Hand] had been onto me at the start of the season that I didn't score enough goals, and to be honest I didn't. He was onto me and onto me about being more ruthless and getting into the box to try and finish off chances.

'Gary Hughes had a great run down the right-hand side and he got to the byline. He looked up, lifted his head and saw me coming — he pulled it back, I let it go across my body and struck it.

'Little did I realise it would be the last goal Limerick scored in Europe. We were very unlucky to go out in the tie 2-1, and in the next round AZ were beaten by Inter Milan, who Liam Brady played with at the time.

'So we were kicking ourselves afterwards thinking we could have had a European Cup Winners' Cup game against Liam Brady's Inter Milan.'

His goal against the Dutch club, as he points out, is still the last goal ever scored by a Limerick player in European competition. And because their glamour tie with Real Madrid was moved to Dublin and they played AZ in the Markets Field, it was also the only European goal scored in Limerick. Ever.

But he doesn't want to dwell on it too much, stating time and time again that he was nothing more than average player who had the good fortune to be a member of a great team.

Instead of boasting about his career, where he marked Maradona, battled Del Bosque, got Kevin Keegan's shirt, played in front of 60,000 at the Santiago Bernabéu, and won the league and FAI Cup, Pat Nolan just speaks about how fortunate he was, and how grateful he is to have the memories he does.

Because that's the word he keeps returning to — memories.

'The memories stay with you and with your family and friends forever,' he repeats.

'It's only in those quiet moments years after you've retired you realise what these games meant to your neighbours and your friends, the lads you went along to the Markets Field with as a kid.

'And it makes the hairs on the back your neck stand up. Medals and trophies and cups and shields and caps and jerseys... they're only immaterial, really. It's memories, and the people you make those memories with, that's what it's all about.

'I'm embarrassed talking about my time in football, to be perfectly honest with you.

'I don't talk about it that much, I wouldn't really, and I haven't spoken about it for a long, long time to anybody. I don't think embarrassment is the word, but I shy away from reflecting on it too much. I very rarely talk about games.

'Someone might bring it up but you just nod and say, 'Ah yeah, yeah,' and move the conversation on. Limerick is a small place. We were just so fortunate to be part of a golden era for football in the area.

'I played for that Limerick jersey. I would have played for nothing. Getting a few bob for it was a bonus. It was always my ambition to play for Limerick, and nothing made me prouder than to play for my boyhood club.

'Winning a league, league cup and an FAI Cup winners' medal alongside your childhood heroes — it's only later on in life you appreciate it and you realise the joy and pleasure that it gave to people. We were the lucky ones.'

FOURTEEN

A TRAGEDY FAR FROM HOME, A GRIEVING COMMUNITY UNITED IN FOOTBALL

—

FINTAN O'TOOLE | 12 MAY

GERRY BOURKE GOT to the Gaelic Grounds in good time before throw-in on 22 July last year.

He'd travelled down to Limerick for the latest chapter in Mayo's whirlwind summer, the Breaffy chairman keen to see the O'Shea brothers and Robbie Hennelly fly the flag for their club.

Getting a good vantage point was not the reason for his early arrival.

It was just over three weeks since David Gavin had gone missing in Canada. He had gotten into difficulty while swimming at Kinbasket Lake in British Columbia.

Despite intensive search efforts there had been no trace of the 25-year-old, a cornerstone in defence for Breaffy football teams over previous years.

There was no sign of the fundraising drive to aid the search for David slowing down. Bourke had arranged to be at the Gaelic Grounds to meet his Crossmolina counterpart Eamon

Howley, who had a donation from his club to be given to the fund, a shining example of how GAA clubs around Mayo had rowed in to support the search.

'I was there and I was hanging around and then this man walks up to me,' said Bourke.

'He says, 'Are you the chairman of Breaffy club?' He'd seen me on the news. I said I was and we shook hands.

'He wanted to sympathise. He asked me to hang on and said don't leave, walked back up to me 15 minutes later and handed me a cheque for €500.

'I don't know who he was or where he was from. He wanted that to go to help to find David's body. This was the type of thing that was happening.

'There are hundreds of tragedies but for some particular reason this hit a nerve with everybody.

'As a club and a community we cannot put our finger on why David Gavin touched so many people in such a sorrowful way.'

Two weeks ago the body of David Gavin was recovered. The search for him had been postponed last October, the plan being to wait until late April when the water levels in the lake would be lowered to facilitate a renewed search.

And a fortnight ago the breakthrough came.

A crew from Calgary were successful at a time when sub aqua clubs and divers from Donegal and Mayo were preparing to travel to Canada to assist in the efforts to find the location of his body.

In February 2017 David emigrated to Canada with his girlfriend Ciara. They settled in Vancouver and he joined the local Gaelic football club.

On 30 June last he was travelling to a GAA tournament in Calgary with team-mates when they decided to stop at

Kinbasket Lake and go for a swim but after jumping in, David got into difficulty as he was making his way to the shore.

Canadian authorities had called off the search in July but the sheer scale of the response to the fundraising efforts in Ireland enabled the search to continue.

'The word came through on the Sunday morning,' recalled Bourke.

'I had got a text, it came through during the night that David had been found. Jesus, it was unbelievable. I went into ten o'clock Mass in Breaffy, the church is right beside me.

'Our own curate Fr McCormack, he was doing a funeral service in Castlebar and we had the parish priest, Fr Eustace. He came out anyway, went up to the altar and welcomed everybody and he said, 'It's a day of celebration, David has been found.'

'The vast majority of the congregation didn't know and there was a gasp in the church. There was joy which is an awful thing to say and is a funny contradiction but there was such joy and relief.

'My own brother and his wife, their daughter was killed in a car accident in 1982. The cemetery is just across the road from their house and I was in the house with them that Sunday evening.

'They said at least now they [the Gavin family] can go to a grave like we can, they can sit down and talk and cry and pray. They have that opportunity now.

'There was huge disappointment last year when Michael and Angela [his parents], their daughter [Aoife] and Ciara [girlfriend] were coming home and there was no body. You were sympathising with them but it was terrible for them.

'At least now they will have a bit of peace.'

Declan Jennings is a Breaffy native, who works as a Games

Promotion Officer with the Garda Westmanstown Gaels club in Dublin. As a player he lined out for Mayo in the 1994 All-Ireland Under-21 final and was a leading light for Breaffy when they were trying to climb out of the junior club ranks.

As a coach he continues to give back to the club. When David graduated from NUI Galway and started working with KPMG in Dublin, he was part of a band of Breaffy players based in the capital that Jennings put through their paces in midweek sessions.

Breaffy's pursuit of the Paddy Moclair Cup still endures and David was central to their recent major attempts at grasping silverware. Corner-back for the 2013 Mayo county senior final loss and wing-back for the 2015 decider defeat.

The October before he emigrated he was full-back as they were edged out by two points in a semi-final by Knockmore.

He had a fine personal Gaelic football CV. In 2009, he was corner-back in the All-Ireland minor final, numbering Cillian O'Connor amongst his Mayo colleagues as they fell three points short in Croke Park against Armagh.

Three years later, there was a Connacht Under-21 season with Mayo and he juggled his studies in Galway with a couple of Sigerson Cup campaigns.

Jennings paints the picture of an elite club player devoted to self-improvement, putting in extra hours outside of the collective sessions.

'If I'd 40 David Gavins, it would make life very easy,' said Jennings.

'He'd be on the phone wanting to know what he could do better or how he could improve. He'd be the first one on the pitch maybe 20 minutes or half an hour before training started. Just an incredible footballer as well.'

'The way he'd come out of the defence with a ball, he just had a bit of class, the way he glided across the ground. A bit like Lee Keegan does, just no effort at all. He was a very important person and team member for those county finals.

'He went away last year and I remember getting a text from him to say he'd be back to training up in Dublin again and he was looking forward to it, maybe in a year's time or whatever.

'He was an extremely intelligent lad and just so bright. A real thinker in lots of ways.'

Breaffy have supplied the O'Shea brothers — Seamus, Aidan and Conor — to the Mayo cause, seen Robbie Hennelly stand between the posts on big Croke Park days and watched players like Michael Hall and Matthew Ruane win All-Ireland U21 medals.

The club's role in the Mayo journey was important to David.

'He was very proud of the lads,' said Jennings.

'I sat beside him at the Mayo and Tipperary All-Ireland semi-final [in 2016]. We were biting our nails when Mayo were scraping across the line. He would have gone to all of the Mayo matches and enjoyed supporting his club men.'

The day after David went missing, it was a message from Aidan O'Shea on the Breaffy team WhatsApp group that informed most in the club of the shocking news across the Atlantic. Later that afternoon, Mayo would get past Derry after extra-time in a qualifier in Castlebar laced with drama.

Both Bourke and Jennings recall the moment when O'Shea notched a vital point, turned and directed his finger towards the sky.

The grief in the club was still raw at the time and the lack of progress in the search deepened the anguish in the coming days.

So they rallied around and did what they could. For the search to be prolonged in Kinbasket Lake, it needed to be funded. The call was issued for help and the response was overwhelming. Money, support and words of comfort flowed in from a wide array of sources.

Some were familiar, like GAA clubs all over Mayo, but acts of generosity came from unknown quarters as well. The fund ultimately topped the $300,000 mark, a staggering reflection of the goodwill created.

Jennings was part of a group collecting outside Cusack Park in Ennis on 8 July when Mayo took on Clare.

'There were about 40 of his friends and team members there. The outpouring of people coming up — I'd never seen anything like it in my life. People throwing in €20, €50, whatever they had and wishing us well.

'It would restore your faith in human kindness. I'll never forget it, it was such a special feeling.'

'It was a GAA driven thing,' said Bourke.

'I'm a member of the Connacht Council as well. There were prayers said to him at a meeting and people walked up to me after to give me envelopes with money in it.

'The amount of goodwill was huge. I'd go into in a match in MacHale Park and people would be asking for him, describing him as one of our own. It really came home to us the impor-tance of the GAA to a community. It resonated with so many.'

The weeks and months from then on in 2017 were difficult to put down, a cloud hanging over the business of keeping a GAA club going.

'It was hard to celebrate wins last year with club or county to be quite honest,' stated Bourke.

'I'd say if we had won the county final — and we were

knocked out early on — it wouldn't have had the same impact on us. There was an air of gloom hanging over the parish and the club. His death had a huge impact on the players in the club and those who would have gone to school with him and in the neighbouring clubs as well.

'It struck a chord with them all. He was such a lovely fella. You could have good footballers who have little personality but Gav like was larger than life. Everybody loved him.'

The club organised a vigil Mass a few days after the accident and later the clubhouse was organised for a memorial where hordes of sympathisers had the opportunity to meet the Gavin family.

It was a strange and sad time as the search was still ongoing thousands of miles away.

'It was shocking to have a memorial and not to have a body,' recalled Bourke.

'Having to meet the family then, oh, it was absolutely terrible. It's something we're not accustomed to.

'I'm sure if you were in America and soldiers had gone to war, you could only get a feel what those parents had gone through and they never have a body.'

The prolonged quest of the Mayo footballers to lift Sam Maguire and the series of recent epic summer journeys which culminate in a loss at Croke Park have tended to prompt words like 'heartbreak' and 'sadness' being tossed about in the post-championship debates.

Last year there was no difficulty to find some perspective in Breaffy.

'You'd see his dad at Breaffy games and you'd just nearly be hoping Gav would be playing for him,' stated Jennings.

'Before you probably would have gone that it's all about

Mayo. We're all caught up in our lives with work and Mayo football, but it just makes you think what happened to him. We were all devastated in Breaffy.

'He was such a positive fella and held in such high respect all over the place. There was just something very special about him the way he held himself. [I'm] very relieved for his family.'

Gerry Bourke is born and bred in Breaffy. He lives in the same house that his grandmother grew up in and where himself and his nine elder siblings were reared.

The chief steward in MacHale Park on match days, tomorrow's Connacht showdown between Mayo and Galway had long been earmarked as a seismic start to the GAA summer.

As club chairman he has been immersed in the preparations for the 'Breaffy OsKaRs' fundraiser they were holding last night.

It's a hectic time but there are regular reminders about a lost son of their club. On Wednesday, Michael Gavin messaged him good wishes from Vancouver for a successful running of the fundraiser.

On Thursday he got a call from an 84-year-old Mayo fan in relation to access to the stadium tomorrow and yet the conversation started with an enquiry as to how the Gavin family were doing.

'It's still there with a lot of people in Mayo. I don't think it'll affect the players, if anything it'll affect them in a positive way. There's a positivity now where there was a negativity last year. He's not lost any more, he's found.'

Declan Jennings is heading back home around lunchtime today, he's planning to take the Breaffy Under-16 team for a training session this evening and then has one of the coveted match tickets for tomorrow. It's been an odd couple of weeks but there's still that sense of anticipation before a big Connacht championship game.

'We're very proud of the lads that play for Mayo from our club. They're immense lads and incredible men for the kids in Breaffy.

'And I know Gav was very proud of them as well. We're very glad that they found him. We can put a bit of closure to it and bring him home.'

PICKING UP THE PIECES AFTER A CAREER SHEDDING BLOOD, SWEAT AND TEARS ON THE PITCH

—

PAUL DOLLERY | 18 MAY

THERE ISN'T A shortage of fond memories for Tony Buckley to recall when he looks back on his playing days.

'One thing I enjoy remembering was a game against South Africa and during it Bakkies Botha was trying to wind me up,' says the former Ireland prop. 'He was trying to goad me into hitting him off the ball, basically. 'Come on, Mushy, I've got you, I'll take you'… all this sort of thing.

'I ignored him and just said to myself that I'd wait for my chance to get the fucker. Later on anyway when he went into a ruck, he looked back and I just tore into him with a shoulder that put him flat on his back.

'I looked down and said to him: 'Well, Bakkies… who's got who now?' He was one of the biggest names in world rugby, someone I admired a lot. It's a small thing, but that's something I can look back on and smile about.'

Four years since his career at the highest level came to an end, Buckley is still dealing with the consequences of over a decade of professional rugby. Surgery has eased his shoulder issues, but his back remains problematic. Recently it forced him to take a month off from his job at Johnson & Johnson in Limerick, where he's tasked with running and maintaining automated production lines.

'With the game the way it is now, pain is a constant,' says the 37-year-old father of three. 'You can't take that many hits and not be in pain. I'm still plagued. My body is destroyed. I was at a neurologist yesterday because of a herniated disc. I'm used to it all by now.'

Buckley can handle the physical pain, he insists. As for the psychological wounds, they're not so easy to ignore.

Meeting the former Ireland international was originally intended as an opportunity to reflect on Munster's last European Cup triumph, the 10-year anniversary of which is this Thursday. The fond memories may be plentiful, but revisiting them can be a complicated process.

'It's a European medal so it was obviously the pinnacle of my career,' says Buckley, who replaced Marcus Horan for the final 17 minutes of Munster's 16-13 victory over Toulouse in the 2008 Heineken Cup final at Cardiff's Millennium Stadium.

'It was a crazy atmosphere and it was amazing to be involved in that with such a great team — the best team in Europe at the time. But you move on. I find it hard to spend too much time looking back. It's something I'd struggle with, to be honest.

'I know I achieved a lot and I can be proud of that. I just try not to look back too much because there's a lot of negative stuff in the past as well. I know that winning the Heineken Cup was a positive thing, but if I think about that then there's a lot of other stuff back there too that wasn't so positive.'

With the benefit of hindsight, Buckley can trace the difficulties he has encountered with his mental health back as far as 2007, just two years after he first joined Munster following a season with Connacht.

He was an 18-stone second-row forward when he first linked up with Shannon after completing his secondary education at Newbridge College. Having undergone surgery on a shoulder problem, he moved home to Newmarket in North Cork to recover. Six months of mammy's cooking and no exercise pushed his weight up to 23 stone.

'There was no way anyone would have been able to lift me in a lineout at that stage.'

When he returned to Shannon after recovering from the injury, Buckley was convinced to move into the front row, where he remained until his professional career ended at Sale Sharks in 2014.

He won 25 caps for Ireland, the last of which he marked with a try against Russia at the 2011 World Cup. With Munster he was a Heineken Cup and Magners League winner. Nevertheless, his career is often remembered as one of unfulfilled potential. It's an assessment he can understand, yet there was much more to it than meets the eye.

Playing rugby for Munster and Ireland gave Buckley a buzz like nothing else could, but regular encounters with illness and injury took a physical and mental toll. A pelvic problem left him weeks away from enforced retirement in 2006. Bouts of glandular fever and pneumonia were among the many other setbacks that hampered his progress.

The positional switches were also burdensome. While his ability in the loose was almost unparalleled for a prop, he was generally playing catch-up in the scrums following his late introduction to life as a front-row forward.

'I had a few consistent, uninterrupted runs at prop during which I felt I did well,' he says. 'But there was always another stumbling block ahead to try and get over. It was fairly tough trying to get through all those to try and play at that level.

'As for playing prop, it can take a lot from your game because you lose so much energy from scrummaging. If your technique isn't as good as it should be — which mine wasn't — then you end up losing even more energy than you should. When you're so tired, trying to function around the field is really hard. It changes your game completely.

'I think I was 20 when I moved to prop, which was quite late to be doing it. Then you're also going from tighthead to loosehead. I lost a lot of years getting turned inside out. I could definitely have done with more hands-on coaching. Greg Feek [Ireland scrum coach] was brilliant and it would have been good to work with him a bit more.'

He adds: 'People talking about unfulfilled potential, that's why I try not to go into the past. People who believe that, they haven't walked any steps in my shoes. When you have so many injuries and illnesses, pains and aches, and you're trying to play every week... I loved playing, I'd be buzzing... but those negatives just take from the love of it. You end up being swallowed up by the negativity.

'That's why I try not to look back, because I don't want to go down the route of wondering about what I should have done or could have done. Of course there are things that could have happened differently but you have to live with those decisions.'

A decisive moment for Buckley occurred in December 2010,

when Munster suffered a 19-15 defeat away to Ospreys which contributed to their failure to reach the knockout stages of the Heineken Cup for the first time in 12 years.

'I was down with the flu all week but I played anyway and made an absolute tit of myself, even though I scored a try,' Buckley explains. 'I was exhausted and made a bollocks of the scrums. After that game, just before Christmas, the IRFU pulled their offer of a new contract.'

Buckley had been on the verge of leaving in the past. Four years earlier, he agreed to join Bath before Munster improved his terms to keep him at home. But this time he was off. There were some attractive offers on the table from abroad, one of which stood out at a time when Buckley's wife — former Ireland international Elaine Collins — was unwell.

Although initially there was frustration over his contract situation with the IRFU, there was a bigger picture to Buckley's decision to sign a three-year deal with Sale Sharks.

He explains: 'My wife was very ill. I had options for clubs, but we went with Sale because it was close to the Christie Hospital in Manchester. There was new research going on there with her treatment so she was in the door early for that. She had an unreal response to it. The rugby didn't go well at Sale but the main reason we went there was so that she could have treatment. The rugby was secondary.'

Buckley made 59 appearances during his three-year spell with the English Premiership club. The final season proved to be particularly challenging as he spent the majority of it on the sidelines due to a broken leg.

A long and lonely period of recovery and rehabilitation did little for his state of mind. By the time his contract expired in the summer of 2014, Buckley — a few months shy of his

34th birthday — ignored offers from France and elsewhere in England to move home.

'I found that last year really, really tough. I was delighted to get back home after it,' says Buckley, who later played a few games of amateur rugby for Kanturk and Shannon before bringing an end to his playing career.

'That [leg] injury finished me eventually but I should have retired anyway. I was in absolute agony. I used to be in the gym every day at 6am, working hard until about 3pm or 4pm. That went on for months. It weighs heavily on the mind then.

'The grá was gone at that stage. Retiring wasn't a big worry for me either. I didn't turn professional until I was nearly 25 so I knew what working life was like from before that. I had worked on sites and stuff. It didn't scare or intimidate me at all. That part of the transition wasn't a problem.

'The overall adjustment was tough. When you're playing professionally, there's a squad of 35 players, a backroom staff, all that support around you. You're in a bubble and everything is taken care of. It takes over your life and controls everything.

'Then when you finish it's just gone completely. The phone stops ringing. This literally happens overnight. You realise fairly quickly that half the friends you had weren't your friends at all. They were just using you for tickets. Half the people I considered friends then haven't spoken to me since I retired. That's the downside of it. That's difficult.'

Buckley underwent counselling to help him tackle the tough times in Sale. There were occasions when he suffered anxiety attacks during games which reduced him to tears on the pitch.

Publicly discussing his battle with depression isn't something he has done before. He doesn't have anything to hide. Media attention just isn't something he's programmed to court. In this instance it came to him with a view to reminiscing about the good old days of the past. Doing so isn't possible for Tony Buckley without acknowledging the difficult days of the present.

Having been diagnosed with major depression, panic disorder and anxiety attacks, Buckley has been receiving weekly treatment for the past year which is gradually bringing him to a better place. He's confident that it will eventually allow recollections of his involvement in World Cups and European Cup finals to flow more easily.

'It's tough, but I'm doing well,' he says. 'This is my first time putting it out there. Depression is something that you don't realise what it is until you have it. It's been going on for years. It's why reminiscing can bring me into a negative spiral of thought. It can be shocking.

'I suppose it's a hard thing to admit to as well. The difficult thing in a lot of ways is that people don't realise what's wrong with them until it goes too far and then it's out of control. It's a scary place to be.

'Mental health services in this country are severely under-funded. Millions of euro are pumped into road safety campaigns but only a fraction of that is spent on mental health. It doesn't seem to be a priority for the government, but the staff in the public sector are brilliant in spite of that.

'The biggest thing is that you have to ask for help, and you have to be careful about who you ask. You have to talk to a professional, not someone who'll just say 'toughen up, you'll be grand'.

'Go to your GP. For players, there's a massive support network there now. They have psychologists and psychiatrists on board with the players' union so they're well in touch there. For other people, tell your GP your story, let that be your starting point.

'Don't just hold it inside, because it won't pass, it will only get worse. It will take over, you'll go to a very dark place and once you're down there it's hard to get out. Speak to someone before you find yourself down there, and remember that it's a lot more common than people think.'

A few hours after our conversation in a Cork café, my phone rings. Tony Buckley is on the other end.

'I just wanted to add a couple of things,' he says. 'I don't want people to think that I didn't enjoy my career at all. That's not what I'm getting at. I have so much good stuff that I can look back on and appreciate.

'I also don't want people to think I have some agenda here. I'm not speaking about this because I'm trying to raise my profile or anything like that. I'll be slipping back into anonymity after this. I didn't come into the interview planning to address this. I just thought I'd raise it while I have the platform, which I'll probably never have again.

'If one person reads this and feels it helps them, that'd be a good thing. That'd be brilliant. That's what it's about. I just wanted to make that clear.'

SIXTEEN

ONE SUMMER IN LONDON: IRISH HOCKEY'S MAGICAL WORLD CUP MOMENT

—

RYAN BAILEY | 18 AUGUST

THE COACH IN question stresses he doesn't swear often, if at all, but few could have blamed him in the circumstances. It happened a couple of years ago now, but the story had suddenly become all the more relevant on the back of the extraordinary events in London — and it neatly summarised the enormity of it all.

Shortly after an Ireland Under-18 girls team — which included a number of players now in the senior side — had been narrowly defeated in the final of an underage tournament by the all-conquering Netherlands, one of the Irish coaching staff, understandably enthused by the performance, remarked: 'Maybe one day we can play you in a final at senior level.'

The Dutch coach, with contempt, was having none of it, completely dismissing any notion that Ireland had a chance of ever getting to their level.

'Oh, I don't think that is possible,' was his snide response, to which the said member of the Irish management replied: 'Why don't you just fuck off?'

So when Ireland lined up alongside the Netherlands for the 2018 Women's World Cup final, you can see why this story had quickly grown legs, becoming another reference point for the remarkable progress of this team.

Whether you were into sport or not, whether you were a hockey fan or not, you couldn't fail to be moved by the occasion, and appreciate the emotions involved. Never had Irish hockey experienced such a day, rarely had Irish sport witnessed an achievement on such a scale.

And with that, the heart burst with pride to watch the Irish hockey fraternity have their time in the spotlight, not because of the Dutch coach's comments but because after years of marginalisation, of near-misses, of fighting tooth and nail for funding, for attention and for respect, they deserved it. They had earned it.

This was their time, and not a moment too soon.

* * *

THERE ARE SPORTING upsets and then there is the story of the Irish women's hockey team at the 2018 World Cup. Never before — in the European Championships, the World Cup or an Olympic Games — had a team ranked so low confounded so many expectations.

Beginning the tournament 16th in the world, Ireland tore the script to shreds, rewrote the history books and entered the hearts and minds of a nation not only with their performances, but the manner in which they carried themselves on the pitch, becoming ambassadors for the country and role models for younger generations.

Nobody had given them a chance. There was no reason to, but the players believed. They believed from the moment they picked themselves up off the canvas three years ago, they believed from the moment they beat a ragged USA side 3-1 on the opening night, and they believed when they had no right to believe.

And then, in that split second, when everything appeared to slow down and Chloe Watkins flicked her effort past the goalkeeper and towards the backboard, Irish hockey was catapulted into uncharted territory. Into dreamland, scaling scarcely-believable and rarefied heights.

A crushed Indian side, defeated and disbelieving, collapsed in the middle of the pitch, forlorn figures in what had become an amphitheatre of screaming green and white.

The Irish team — standing shoulder-to-shoulder, hand-in-hand on the halfway line — dispersed in pandemonium, some charging in one direction, others throwing their sticks and stampeding towards Watkins in the other. Nobody quite knew what to do, yet it mattered little. All logic, all reason, had gone out the window.

Graham Shaw, the head coach, unable to watch the penalty shootout, glanced skywards and, in releasing his emotions after the unbearable stress and tension of a World Cup quarter-final, let his guard down for the first time. The gratification etched all over his face.

'I don't even remember what happened because a couple of my team-mates said they ran straight towards me and I actually ran away from them, I didn't even seen them,' Watkins says, looking back on that match-winning moment.

'It was just an absolute blur, I don't even know what happened. I think I threw my stick and everything went out the window. It was one of the best moments of my hockey career, of my life.'

Amid the utter disbelief, there were tears in the stands. Most in green had personal connections with the team, the family and friends who have lived through the crushing lows and exhilarating highs down through the years. Mothers, fathers, brothers, sisters, uncles, aunts, cousins. You could feel the pride, and see the raw, unadulterated emotion.

'I have never been as proud to be Irish,' Gordon Watkins, Chloe's father and a former international, smiles. 'Never in my wildest dreams... never in my lifetime did I ever think anything like it was possible.'

But it was no fluke, rather years in the making. Years of hurt, of setbacks, of sacrifice, of agony, of persevering and campaigning when nobody was listening, or cared. That's what it's like to be invested in a minority sport in Ireland. It's tough work, but the rewards make it all worth it.

'You've got to endure the lows to appreciate the highs, don't you?' Gordon continues.

'I said to Chloe after Valencia [when Ireland lost a shootout to miss out on Olympic qualification] to be brave enough to step up and do it. Don't stand back and watch something happen that you can't change or do anything about. To have the confidence to do it.

'I just thought to myself, 'Go on, Chloe. You can do it. I know you can."

* * *

SOMETIMES, WHEN ACHIEVEMENT is contextualised, and pain has preceded triumph, it just means more.

Because behind every success story is an emotionally-charged journey, often a white-knuckle ride of highs and lows, joy and despair and moments in time when the flame flickered. When the term 'near miss' becomes plural. When that thread of optimism threatened to snap, but never did because there was always that one ambition driving it forward.

Sport does that, no matter the level. It takes and takes, but will always recompense. Tears are par for the course, but the rewards will always outweigh the sacrifices. Even if it's for one fleeting moment of glory. Of success. Of vindication. It's always worth it.

'There were times you do think of walking away,' Chloe admits. 'You do think that because as amateur athletes you dedicate your life to the cause and because the tough times weigh heavy, there's only so much you can take.

'You begin to question your life — can I keep doing this?'

But just as Ireland's men used the anguish of a succession of near misses to turn the tide and change the culture within the dressing room to qualify for the Rio Olympics, the women's national team travelled a strangely similar pilgrimage — the ledger would contain wildly oscillating peaks and troughs — to reach the heady promised land of a first World Cup in 16 years.

For that reason, this summer was always going to feel like a seminal moment for Irish hockey, but particularly for this team under Shaw, who was the man tasked with picking up the pieces and rebuilding after the Rio qualification campaign ended in utter heartbreak.

It wasn't the first time this group of players had fallen so agonisingly at the final hurdle — the 2012 Olympic dream came crashing down in similarly cruel circumstances — but hitting rock bottom can so often be the turning of the tide.

That excruciatingly painful defeat to China in June 2015 — when the width of a post separated delirium and despair — ended the Rio dream, and at the same time, the hopes of many who had longed to represent Ireland on the big stage. 'I saw them coming out after playing China and literally, they had to be helped physically to the bus,' Gordon recalls. 'Some of them were physically distraught, they could hardly walk such was the devastation. I've no doubt if they went out to play an Under-12 team the next day, they would have lost. They were absolutely gone mentally and physically. Just crushed.'

Was there any coming back from that?

'I think we all reassessed,' Chloe says. 'You look at another two- or four-year cycle and it's a long time. Getting up at 5.30am to go to the gym before work and getting in late after training that night.

'I think it actually hit my family more. They nearly feel worse, because they know what you go through and they see you committing everything to it. I know my Mum, it took her months to get over Rio.

'Personally, I questioned it but we all knew we had the talent to do it and achieve something special. We knew we could do it and we were so close. It was just about resetting, rediscovering the motivation and committing together as a group.

'I'm glad I didn't throw in the towel and I was able to give my family something to cheer about and a more positive experience this time around. We had come off second best enough [times], so to do what we did made it even more special.'

* * *

IRELAND SHOULD NEVER have stood a chance at this World Cup, but here they were on the most glorious of summer's days in the shadows of London's Olympic Stadium bringing the nation on an unexpected sporting journey, disrespecting theirs and everybody else's world ranking and placing themselves among the protagonists of the game.

A tight-knit group of students, lawyers, doctors and teachers embarking on a magical odyssey over the most enchanting and fulfilling two weeks of their lives and in the history of Irish hockey. Perhaps even Irish sport.

Shaw has been instrumental in the team's development and it's no coincidence that the qualities he had as a player quickly became fundamental principles within the four walls of a dressing room with an enviable bond and togetherness. An unrelenting work ethic, a never-say-die attitude, a no-excuses mantra.

In dispatching higher-ranked USA, India and Spain en route to the final and a historic silver medal, this team showed that if the right attitude and sacrifice is there, there are no limitations to what can be achieved. And therein lies the beauty of sport, the allure of the unexpected. When the impossible becomes possible.

'The first game of the tournament, against USA, just settled everyone,' Chloe says.

'Even Graham said it to us, it just set us up and gave us such confidence. He could see when Deirdre [Duke] scored we were at it and then we just built up so much momentum and suddenly after two wins, we were in the quarter-final.

'We were aware of what was going on at home and the buzz that was building, but were just so focused on seizing the opportunity and turning to the next game. We just wanted it so much so all of the outside stuff spurred us on, rather than got us carried away.

'The morning after the quarter-final, we were going down to mobility [training] and Graham turned to us and kind of just said, 'We had a great day yesterday but we have a World Cup semi-final to prepare for,' and from that point on, everyone just settled down and didn't let anything distract us.

'It wasn't like we have got this far, so whatever happens happens. It was like we have got this far, we have worked so hard for this, and we're not going to let it slip by. We were in a World Cup semi-final, representing our country and playing with our best friends. We had waited so long for this chance.'

* * *

IT BECAME CLEAR very quickly that demand far exceeded supply, but even with tickets being like gold dust, that didn't stop large swathes of Irish supporters decamping en masse to the Olympic Park.

The World Cup fan village turned into a sea of green from early in the day as the Irish diaspora in London were joined by thousands who had embarked on last-minute, early-morning trips from home to witness a piece of sporting history.

It was a case of trains, planes and automobiles for many as they scrambled to get over to London in time for the semi-final against Spain, with a large portion of the support travelling over without tickets, simply desperate to be part of the occasion in whatever way they could.

Gordon Watkins had rented an apartment for the duration of the tournament, which at a cost of nearly €2,000 may have seemed expensive at first, but turned out to be an inspired decision.

He, along with several other parents, had been an ever-present in the stands throughout, living and breathing every minute as if he was out there himself; it meant just as much to the parents, the volunteers, the club players, the team-mates, the umpires, the officials and the past players as it did to the 18 players in green.

'I've never experienced anything like it,' he says. 'I never thought I would either and I was getting texts from all over the world, from people I used to play with or against. I think I got 900 texts in four days. Everybody realised something special was happening.'

Gareth Watkins, Chloe's older brother and a former men's international, had flown over and back for the pool game against India, but had to quickly readjust his plans when Ireland advanced into the quarter-finals.

'Everyone was chatting about what we were going to do as the quarter-final was on the Thursday, which wasn't ideal with work, but then my boss was just like, 'It's a World Cup quarter-final, take two days off and get back over to London.'

'And then we win the quarter and you're thinking, 'Christ, we can't go home now.' I had planned to go on holidays with my girlfriend for the August bank holiday weekend but rang home pretty quickly and asked her what about coming to London for the weekend instead of Cork. It was all a bit mad.'

With both the semi-final and final sold-out as fans of other nations had pre-booked seats in anticipation of their team being involved at that stage of the tournament, Gordon spearheaded the search for tickets.

'I was inundated with people asking me,' he laughs. 'Thankfully I had met an Aussie who had block-booked tickets for the Australian brigade but obviously they didn't make it through.

He said he had 30, possibly 50, tickets for the semi and the same for the final so I said to him, 'Don't go to anyone else, we'll take all of them.'

'I arranged to meet him after the quarter-final, behind the goal at the bar, and Joan from Hockey Ireland liaised with him and started allocating the tickets to all the families and friends and Irish support.

'To see the stadium decked out in green for the semi and final was just amazing and I know it lifted the girls so much.'

***

SUNDAY, 5 AUGUST 2018.

'I don't think I'll ever forget that day,' Chloe, with a silver medal around her neck, laughs, still in a state of bewilderment.

After their post-match semi-final media requirements were fulfilled, and the players had eventually found their way onto the team bus, there was little time to reflect on the absurdity of what had just happened.

'Obviously I'll always remember the quarter-final, but the semi-final topped it again,' she says. 'It was just bonkers, we were living our dream. I had to turn my phone on to airplane mode because it was just exploding.

'I had to turn it off because we had to sleep, we had to recover, as we had a World Cup final — how mad is that? — the next day. We all had to delete social media apps off our phones just to make them calm down a bit. I don't think I touched my phone before the final, because I literally couldn't start responding to people.

'It was amazing to hear from people you haven't spoken to in years because they're sending you lovely messages saying how proud they are of you. Those were the moments when you kind of realised the impact it was having.'

A World Cup final? Surreal the players kept saying, simply unable to fully process what had happened.

'I was rooming with Ayeisha [McFerran] and we went to bed on the Saturday night and I think about 10 minutes after we turned the lights off, she burst out laughing — 'Are we actually playing in a World Cup final tomorrow?' — and the two of us were just laughing for about 10 minutes and then had to calm down again and go to bed.

And it was a bit like that on the Sunday morning, everyone was kind of looking around. Nobody was nervous because I think we were all in a state of shock.

'At random times people just burst out laughing because it was like, 'Hang on here, what have we done?' and especially because we were in a hotel with other teams that let's just say weren't too happy with the outcome of their tournament. It kind of made it a bit nicer walking around the hotel in your Irish top.'

And then, somehow, they had to refocus for the game that they dreamed of playing in for their entire lives. Ireland versus the Netherlands — the seven-time champions, the standard-bearers — in a World Cup final in front of 10,000 fans and a TV audience of millions.

'Sharpie started that meeting, the pre-World Cup final meeting, and we all kind of sat down and there was a moment's pause,' Chloe remembers. 'We were looking around at each other smiling and laughing and then we were like right, everyone was writing in their notebook 'World Cup final versus Netherlands' and then taking notes. It was a bit surreal.'

Afterwards, an element of disappointment was only natural as the curtain came down on the groundbreaking campaign with a heavy defeat to the Dutch, but it could take nothing away from what a group of 18 amateur athletes had achieved.

The result left Shaw's side with mixed emotions at full-time, but the outcome provided delight for both teams, as Ireland's deflation quickly turned to elation as they collected their silver medals in front of the Green Army.

'We were the last team to leave the pitch after the ceremony. We just wanted to soak it all up, savour every minute. The support was incredible, they were moments you'll just never forget. And then you go out afterwards and meet your family and friends, and to bring the medal out to them... to see what it meant was incredible.'

For Gordon, that's when it really hit home.

'They were coming out one-by-one,' he recalls. 'That was the emotional part. Just an experience that you'd love to live all over again, but so grateful that we got to experience it in the first place.'

* * *

THERE ARE TOO many highlights to pick out as a favourite, too many memories to condense into one answer. The moments of theatre from the 23-line which earned shootout wins over India and Spain are obvious choices, as is the final and the homecoming on Dame Street, but what stands out most for Chloe Watkins are the smaller, behind-closed-doors, moments which the players will always hold onto, and cherish.

Ireland hit some historic landmarks along the way, the exploits of the group eclipsing what had gone before, and most significantly overachieving when the baggage of under-achievement had previously weighed them down.

There had been tantalising glimpses of what could be achieved down through the years, one-off victories over higher-ranked nations, but never had they truly fulfilled their full potential on the big stage. All of those demons were banished, history rewritten.

'There were a couple of little things that just spurred us on,' she explains. 'After the quarter-final, we all came back to the hotel and you needed to use your room key to work the lift. One of the girls said hers wasn't working, so someone else took theirs out and it didn't work either.

'We quickly realised the keys no longer worked as we were only checked into the hotel until that day, so we all had to go down and get our keys renewed. It was just funny and gave us a little bit more motivation.

'And it was funny when we were leaving for the tournament, you'd get stopped in Dublin airport and people would ask, 'Oh, what team are you?' because they'd see the top. And we'd explain we're the hockey team and we're going to the World Cup. They had no idea but would wish us luck or whatever. Two of the girls were getting onto the plane and messing, turned around on the steps and waved to the crowd that wasn't there, kind of saying, 'We're off now.'

'Two weeks later, we arrived back in Dublin and it was the complete opposite... we had the fire brigade with tricolours escorting us off the runway, we went through the side exit of the airport and were greeted by thousands of people and then you have people taking pictures of our bus through town.

'Everybody was literally thinking, 'What is going on?' We were in an area in town we knew wasn't a hockey area yet here are all these people. You could just never have imagined anything like it in your wildest dreams. Ever.'

202 | BEHIND THE LINES

It may take some time for the enormity of the achievement and the ripple effect it will have on the sport in this country to be fully processed by those involved, but for now the players and their families continue to savour every minute of the most extraordinary summer.

'People are constantly asking me, 'Are you proud of your sister, are you proud of your sister?' Gareth adds. 'Of course I'm always going to be proud of her because she's my sister but it's so fantastic to see someone who I know has put in every hour realise her dream on the big stage.

'To see my sister go to a World Cup and not suffer the heartbreak that had been associated with this team for so long, but to go out and enjoy it and achieve what they achieved. That's what made it, to see the sheer joy it gave people. We'll never forget that.'

Sometimes, it just means more.

—

SEVENTEEN

IN MEMORY OF MY MOTHER; FOOTBALL, FAMILY AND FINDING COMFORT IN THE PAST

—

EOIN O'CALLAGHAN | 15 JULY

ON 27 MAY, my Mum died suddenly.

A few days later, I was standing in her bedroom and staring into her wardrobe. It was filled with colour and style and vibrancy and my eyes began to sting.

I stood there for a long time. I smelled her clothes and held them in my hands. Everything was the same. Everything. On her bedside locker was her portable radio with an elastic band wrapped around it. There was a box of Tic Tacs. There were photos from my wedding two years ago. Everything was the same. But it wasn't.

What I noticed most after her death was the silence. As a family, you bind together at difficult moments. You swap stories and reminisce and laugh hard, usually at very inappropriate things. And when there's a death, you get so many visitors. There's a constant din, an electricity of interaction. You're always entertaining. But then the silence comes and it gets you in the gut. You're not even aware of it but you begin to stare into space a lot, unable to speak. You want to speak but the words just don't come out, like stepping on the accelerator with the handbrake on. So, you sit and wait for someone else to deal with the silence better than you can.

And as I stood there, in the silence of my Mum's bedroom, I realised the finality of it. I realised that there would always be a silence from now on.

My Dad asked if I wanted to take anything of Mum's with me and there was. A medal that belonged to my grandfather and that she proudly wore on the lapel of one of her winter coats. She had attached a pin to the back of it so it looked like a brooch and for years I examined it up close. It was gold, engraved with the Munster crest and given to my grandfather in 1926 for winning the Munster Football League 2nd Division. On the back, it was personalised with the words 'D. DUNLEA (CAPT)'. Underneath, some more detail: 'Won by ST VINCENT'S A.F.C.'

Whenever Mum wore the coat, she'd point to the medal and encourage me to inspect it, as if it was the first time I was seeing it. I'd ask some questions about my grandfather's football career but Mum didn't seem to know much. She said that he served a ban for playing a garrison sport and that was about it. She didn't have any detail on St. Vincent's or the Munster Football League. But she loved that medal. She loved showing it off. She was so proud of her father.

Before Mum died, I never thought about that medal. I knew it existed but was ignorant to its story. I didn't care enough to ask Mum about it in greater detail. I never sat down and asked her about her family, what her parents were like, if she ever saw her father play football or what position he played.

I've covered football for 12 years now. Maybe my Mum

hoped that one day I'd temporarily ignore the Premier League and the World Cup and write about our own family's connection to the game that I loved so much. But I never did.

I live in Toronto and on the plane journey back home, I stared into space a lot. I thought about the medal and its significance. It wasn't really about my grandfather anymore. It was about my Mum. It was about a basic thing I had failed to do when she was still alive: taking an interest.

I wanted to know more about that medal and my grandfather.

Some details I already had thanks to census records and my own father's impeccable memory.

Daniel Dunlea was born in 1905, the youngest child of Bartholomew and Mary, and raised in Sunday's Well on the northside of Cork City. He had one brother — Martin — and two sisters, Nora and Molly. There had been more children — seven in total — but three had died as infants.

Later, he became a familiar presence to local dwellers. He was responsible for delivering to the various watering holes in the city and there's even a picture of him — probably snapped sometime in the 1950s — perched on his horse at Patrick's Bridge, the reins gripped tightly in his hands and the precious cargo stored in the cart behind him. He's wearing a shirt, tie, blazer and a tilted trilby on his head. Around him, the bicycles and pedestrians go by. But the way the image is framed, Daniel is a striking, imposing and memorable figure.

Also, it's a rare collector's item. A photograph of my grandfather and a window — however tiny — into who he was.

When I was little, I'd always sit next to my Mum at mass. Bored, I'd stare at the altar and the two pillars on either side. I'd imagine them as goalposts and how I'd outfox the goalkeeper/priest with an expertly curled shot to the far corner.

Later, but still bored, there were other things that passed more time.

Mum would always bring her own missal to church. It had a navy cover and was filled with memorial cards of friends and family. Always, I'd take them out and flick through them. The cards were all identical, as if everybody got them done in the same place. On the front was a photograph with the person's name, age and their date of death. On the back, there was always some biblical verse or a poem. Some faces — the younger ones — I recognised. And others I didn't.

The majority of people in the photographs seemed so old, their faces hardened. And the ones I always seemed to focus on were my grandparents.

I never met any of them. To me, they were mythical, curious figures. Growing up, you'd hear references but that was it. You could see them in my parents' wedding album but they were almost lost in the crowd. I do remember looking at both my grandfathers — resplendent in their top hats and tails in the mid-1960s — and drawing an immediate contrast. My Dad's father wore glasses and seemed smaller, almost diminutive. Daniel was bald but tall and debonair. There appeared a breezy elegance. An assurance to the way he carried himself.

There were other aspects of his life that I knew about. I knew he married Molly and they had two girls — Mary was the oldest and then Joan, my Mum, came along a few years later. I knew they lived above a bakery. I knew they went to deepest, darkest west Cork on their honeymoon and loved it so much that, ever since, three generations of our family have been immersed in Union Hall and its surrounding areas since birth. I knew that Molly referred to her husband as Danny.

But, up until my Mum's death, that was about it. Afterwards, some new fragments of information came to light. Mum, a classical music buff, had long wondered about a certain piece of music her father used to sing as a party piece. She remembered the melody but not the name until one day several years ago when she heard Toselli's Serenade on Lyric FM.

And on her final journey at The Island Crematorium, she was accompanied by Mario Lanza who serenaded her with that song the entire way.

In the subsequent days and weeks, I learned more about Danny.

Thanks to Plunkett Carter, the esteemed historian and authoritative voice on Cork football history, I found out just how much of a talented footballer my grandfather was.

Danny played the game in the immediate aftermath of the Civil War, the era of the Irish Free State. Inevitably, in the early years of organised soccer (the Munster Football Association was initially formed in 1901), the presence of British soldiers in particular pockets of the country led to various clubs being formed. Writing in Cork Soccer Memories, Plunkett paints an incredible picture of what local sport was like at a time when atmosphere was fraught and rivalry went far beyond what happened on the pitch.

'Soccer was, at the time, very popular in Sunday's Well which was then a very strong nationalist area,' he writes.

'Before hurling became the leading sport in the area, the nationalistic sports enthusiasts gave vent to their feelings on the soccer field where Vincent's often took on Barrackton Utd, a team composed mainly of British soldiers stationed in Cork and naturally loyalist in political outlook.

'There was a famous occasion in the Camp Field when the game was drawing to a close with the teams level at two-all, and a Barrackton forward gained possession and broke through the Vincent's defence. He had only the goalie to beat when he hesitated to pick his spot. Just as he was about to shoot, a Vincent's supporter, sensing the danger, suddenly produced a revolver and shot the ball! That ensured that the game ended in a draw and the honour of Vincent's remained untarnished.'

Before the first World War, the military sides dominated Munster junior football. Barrackton won the provincial Tyler Cup twice in a decade while the likes of Royal Artillery and Haulbowline - where the British Navy had a base — were also victorious.

But, in the 1920s, the most successful junior team was St. Vincent's, captained by my grandfather.

Playing in green and black, the club was only founded in 1922 — the same year the Munster Football Association was reformed — and while the Civil War still raged. Vincent's disbanded just a decade later but, between 1926 and 1929, they managed to claim three Munster titles and reach a national decider: the equivalent of today's FAI Junior Cup final.

The medal my Mum wore so proudly on her lapel was from the 1926 Munster victory over Limerick outfit Dalcassians. But Danny didn't just captain Vincent's to provincial crowns. He was also skipper for the Free State Junior Cup clash against Dublin side Brunswick in 1926.

Over the last few weeks, I'd wake to various emails from the intrepid and dedicated Plunkett, who sat in front of dizzying microfilm units, spooled through various newspaper archive and copied anything of relevance pertaining to my grandfather.

He even sent on a photograph of him.

It was taken before that Free State final in 1926. Danny is in the back-row, fourth from the left. Three things stand out: the beauty of the striped jerseys, his height (he's the tallest on the team) and also the way he drapes his arms around his team-mates on either side, something nobody else is doing. As captain, perhaps he was merely leading by example. But, what struck me as I tried to decipher as much as I could, was that my grandfather was just 21 at the time and still handed the armband. Despite his lack of years, his personality clearly lent itself to leadership. Others looked to him for inspiration.

Despite the game taking place at the Victoria Cross grounds in Cork, Vincent's lost. Over 5,000 fans were in attendance, including a substantial Brunswick crowd who, according to the press report, 'travelled by special train from the metropolis'.

Vincent's attackers came in for criticism but Danny, operating as a fullback, was praised for his performance. The game was decided by a solitary goal and it came from one of Vincent's own players. After a decent start, it set them back considerably.

'Up to the time of this score, the Cork team was much the more aggressive, but the unfortunate reverse damped their ardour to a considerable extent,' went the match description, sitting curiously alongside a death notice of a Denis Healy from Dunmanway and the stock market updates from America.

Still, the defeat was an early indicator of Cork junior teams' difficulties on the national stage. The competition has been running since 1924 and only a handful of Leeside clubs have ever won the trophy. Damningly, the most recent was Rockville in 1945 and no Cork team has even reached the final in over 30 years.

So, the mere fact Vincent's qualified for the 1926 showdown was a relative triumph.

Danny was an excellent defender and his performances for Vincent's ensured he also represented Munster in a Junior Interprovincial clash against Leinster in the mid-1920s.

Alongside ads for the Cork & Kerry Creamery Company and the super-silk Mattamac coat ('favourably known and worn all over the World'), was the team announcement in the local press and Danny was one of four Vincent's players selected to represent the province.

But, the timing was more than a little curious. The game against Leinster took place on a Sunday, 24 hours after Danny and his Vincent's team played a local cup final against Victoria Celtic. Given the circumstances (two Celtic players were also involved), it was understandable that Munster suffered a 3-1 loss but Danny's defensive prowess was again noted.

Vincent's won Munster titles again in 1927 and 1929 but there wouldn't be another march towards national success.

I'm not sure when Danny decided to step away from soccer or when he served a ban but he'd already accomplished so much so quickly. It wasn't long before he married and started a family and his priorities probably changed. By the time my Mum was born, it was already over a decade since the Free State final and certainly a distant memory for him.

But, he was proud of the accomplishment. He was so proud that he kept onto that medal.

And he passed on his love for the game to his family.

Even to this day, my Dad isn't a particularly keen sports fan. He's much too active to sit down and dedicate two hours of his day to a match. He could be doing important things like painting the house or cutting the grass. He'll watch the news and listen to the radio and hear the main headlines. He'll try his best and offer basic updates when I call but my Mum always prided herself on her in-depth knowledge of Cork sports history.

Before marrying my father, she worked in the iconic

Matthews sports store and she'd regale you with stories of watching Raich Carter down the Mardyke in 1953 and how wonderful it was to see Noel Cantwell lift the FA Cup as Manchester United captain a decade later. Usually, she'd also veer into some tale of how Cantwell was an old friend and if I remembered the Cantwells who lived on Redemption Road (I never did) because they were related.

She'd tell you about all the nights spent in the company of lifelong friends Joe and Noreen Hartnett on the Commons Road and how Christy Ring, who she adored, would regularly drop by for tea and chats.

She'd discuss, at length, the inner-workings of the Cork Hibs side managed by Dave Bacuzzi and the wizardry of Dave 'Wiggy' Wigginton. Later, she loved Dave Barry and how he brought such a local quality to Cork City in the mid-90s. She was immensely proud when the team's left-back Gareth Cronin, the son of another good friend, came to our house regularly to get some extra accountancy tutorials from my brother.

After accumulating the research on my grandfather and flicking through everything, I wondered what my Mum would have thought about Danny's football profile. The wins, the accolades, the praise. But she never really cared too much about that stuff. She liked to impress, certainly. But for her, it was important to be well-read, intelligent, sharp and always elegant. For her, quality was never to be measured in trophies.

And then I came across one local columnist and his views on various Vincent's players. For him, Danny Dunlea — my grandfather — was a player 'of style'.

She would've loved that.

EPILOGUE

'I told Fergie to shove his Manchester United contract'
Paul Dollery (22 APRIL)
A Limerick native, Joe Hanrahan earned a shot at the big time with Manchester United, though he always had his business qualifications to fall back on. He ultimately made his mark on the pitch with clubs like Dundalk and Derry City before settling into a successful career in financial services in Dublin.

As part of our League of Ireland legends series, Paul Dollery caught up with the former FAI Cup winner and fan favourite.

—

He could see his house from jail and planned his UFC tilt
from a caravan in Dublin Gavan Casey (11 MARCH)
They're gym-mates, but John Phillips isn't living the Conor McGregor lifestyle yet. Gavan Casey met the fighter who's living in a caravan outside his Dublin gym as he tried to make his mark in the world of MMA. Charting a journey from a Welsh boxing ring to a stint in prison and then Dublin, Phillips has endured lots of false starts in his career.

The 32-year-old tasted another setback the week after this piece ran in March; he succumbed to an opening round choke from Charles 'Kid Dynamite' Byrd at UFC Fight Night 127 in London.

*Night Games: Getting to the heart of toxic masculinity
in sport Paul Fennessy* (20 APRIL)
Irish rugby players Paddy Jackson and Stuart Olding and their
friends Blane McIlroy and Rory Harrison were found not guilty
of all counts after a 42-day trial and 40 minutes of deliberation in
March. Then-Ulster and Ireland No 10 Jackson was charged with
one count of rape and one count of sexual assault; his teammate
Olding was also charged with one count of rape. McIlroy was
accused of one count of exposure and Harrison faced a charge
of perverting the course of justice and withholding information.

Jackson and Olding were dismissed by the IRFU and went
on to secure contracts with clubs in France. The so-called
Belfast Rape Trial and the treatment of the 21-year-old woman
at the centre of the allegations prompted many conversations
throughout the country. Paul Fennessy spoke to Anna Krien,
author of 'Night Games', an award-winning book which
focused on the trial of a young AFL player for rape, about
consent, toxic masculinity, locker room cultures and more.
A version of this interview was first published on 20 April.

—

*Capsizes and calm: Damian Browne's epic solo row across
the Atlantic Sean Farrell* (25 FEBRUARY)
Damian Browne completed the Atlantic Challenge rowing race
in February. The Galway native played for Connacht, Leinster,
Northampton, Brive and Oyannax during a long professional
rugby career at second row.

Now retired, the 4,800km journey from the Canary
Islands to Antigua took Browne 63 days. Back on dry land
he discussed the physical and mental challenges he faced
along the way with Sean Farrell.

The lost genius of Irish football: Remembering Liam Whelan, Dublin's Busby Babe Ryan Bailey (5 FEBRUARY)
To mark the 60th anniversary of the Munich air disaster that claimed the lives of 23 people, including eight of Manchester United's famous Busby Babes, Ryan Bailey remembered his great-uncle: Cabra's Liam Whelan, who was just 22 when he died on that tragic day.

Told with the help of Liam's brothers Christy and John, it is the story of a young star ascendant and on the cusp of greatness, a majestic Irish football talent taken far too soon, and the devastating impact which his death had on the Whelan family.

The article was shortlisted for 'Best Feature' at the 2018 FAI Communication Awards.

—

'I took all the money out of the house, all our wages, and gambled it all in 28 minutes'
Sinéad Farrell (9 DECEMBER 2017)
In November 2017, just two months after they finally reached the promised land and clinched the All-Ireland title, the Dublin Ladies footballers told their story in the acclaimed documentary, 'Blues Sisters'.

One person from the Dubs' backroom whose story didn't feature on the small screen was kitman Willy O'Connor. He spoke to Sinéad Farrell about the devastating gambling addiction that started aged 10 and left his life in ruins and how, at the age of 39, he has found purpose in sport and rebuilt his life.

The day Katie Taylor took on the boys of Ballyfermot
Eoin O'Callaghan (13 JANUARY)
Long before Katie Taylor boxed her way to an Olympic gold medal and a professional world title, she was one of the top footballers in the country, good enough to represent Ireland at senior international level.

In January a clip of Taylor, aged 12, playing schoolboy football for Wicklow club Newtown Juniors was posted online and quickly went viral. Eoin O'Callaghan tracked down the man on the other end of one of Taylor's crunching tackles, Kenny Hammond, to ask him about that day on The Lawns in Ballyfermot.

—

'I look down the back of the bus and there's Claw, fag in his mouth, puffing away' Murray Kinsella (13 JUNE)
During Ireland's successful tour of Australia last summer, Murray Kinsella used the time between Tests to go on a busman's holiday and catch up with a Munster legend.

John Langford is often referenced by the likes of Ronan O'Gara and Paul O'Connell as a huge influence on Munster in the early days of professionalism.

The lock joined the province in 1999 in the nascent days of the Heineken Cup era and featured in the European final defeat to Northampton in 2000. He left the province in 2001 and went on to win a handful of Wallabies caps.

Murray got back on the road and Joe Schmidt's Ireland recorded an historic 2-1 series win Down Under.

Teenage kicks: from Kildare GAA to the Premier League
Ben Blake (14 APRIL)
In April, Liverpool manager Jurgen Klopp named Irish teenager Conor Masterson in his matchday squads for the Reds' Champions League clash against Manchester City as well as the Merseyside derby against neighbours Everton.

Ben Blake spoke to two men who have witnessed the 19-year-old's rise for themselves: Celbridge GAA coach Gerry Kearns and Lucan United coach John Doyle.

Masterson was on the Liverpool bench for both games but, at the time of writing, is yet to make his first-team debut.

—

Silver Saturday as Ireland's young sprinters take on the world
Emma Duffey (10 SEPTEMBER)
Ireland's women's 4 x 100m relay stormed to a historic silver medal at the IAAF Wold Under-20 Championships in Finland in July.

Emma Duffey spoke to her four Irish heroes — Molly Scott, Gina Akpe-Moses, Ciara Neville and Patience Jumbo-Gula — to relieve the dramatic final.

—

One last game on a hospital ward for two old friends and fierce competitors Kevin O'Brien (11 NOVEMBER 2017)
Jim Stynes left Dublin as a skinny 18-year-old for Australia in 1987. He became an icon in the AFL and a huge public figure outside of the oval.

The Dubliner played for over a decade, winning the Brownlow Medal — the game's highest individual honour.

He led Australian sides against his home country in various compromise rules series and went on to become president of the Melbourne club and a director of a foundation for young people.

Stynes, a husband to Sam and father of two young children, was diagnosed with cancer in 2009 and died at the age of 42. AFL legend Garry Lyon, a teammate of Stynes, remembers his good friend in a conversation with Kevin O'Brien in the days before the International Rules Series of November 2017. Hosts Australia won both Tests and recorded a 116-103 aggregate victory.

—

Net loss as Scott Evans hangs up his badminton racket
Steve O'Rourke (7 FEBRUARY)
Ireland's number one badminton player Scott Evans announced his retirement in February, calling time on a career which saw him proudly represent his country at three Olympic Games, making history in the process.

The Dubliner, 30, spoke to Steve O'Rourke about the highs and lows of his life on the court, and about badminton's ongoing struggle for mainstream coverage and meaningful funding in Ireland.

—

The Limerick lad who marked Maradona and battled Real
Madrid in the European Cup Aaron Gallagher (5 AUGUST)
Pat Nolan had never told his full story until he chatted to Aaron Gallagher about winning the Premier Division and FAI Cup with Limerick, playing against Real Madrid in Europe and being tasked with marking Diego Maradona as part of our weekly League of Ireland Legends series.

A tragedy far from home, a grieving community united in football Fintan O'Toole (12 MAY)

In June 2017, David Gavin, a young Gaelic footballer from County Mayo, got into difficulty while swimming in Canada and drowned. Despite an extensive search and recovery mission, the 25-year-old's body remained missing until April 2018 when it was finally recovered and flown home for a funeral in his native Breaffy.

Fintan O'Toole spoke to Breaffy GAA chairman Gerry Bourke and club member Declan Jennings about the tragic loss and the closure which the discovery of David's body brought to a community united in grief.

—

Picking up the pieces after a career shedding blood, sweat and tears on the pitch Paul Dollery (18 MAY)

Paul Dollery sat down with former Munster prop Tony Buckley as the 10th anniversary of the province's 2008 Heineken Cup triumph approached. The conversation quickly veered away from the expected reminiscences on Buckley's life in red and the cast of larger than life characters with whom he shared the dressing room.

Instead, Buckley steered the interview towards his history of injury and illness, publicly discussing his battle with depression for the very first time.

One summer in London: Irish hockey's magical World Cup moment Ryan Bailey (18 AUGUST)
With only one other team ranked beneath them, nobody gave Ireland much of a chance at the Women's Hockey World Cup in London this summer. Nobody, that is, except for the players themselves.

What followed was an incredible journey that captured the hearts of the nation and propelled their sport onto the front pages as the Green Army continually defied all odds, in heart-stopping fashion, to take their place in the World Cup final against seven-time world champions The Netherlands.

In the aftermath of Ireland's silver medal success, Ryan Bailey spoke to three members of the Watkins family — shootout star Chloe, as well as her father Gordon and her brother Gareth, both former internationals themselves — to relive this unforgettable adventure.

—

In memory of my Mother; football, family and finding comfort in the past Eoin O'Callaghan (15 JULY)
After his Mum passed away, Eoin O'Callaghan began to look into his grandfather's football career in 1920s Cork. Determined to unearth the story of how a medal — a favourite of his mother's — was won, Eoin traces the progress of Daniel Dunlea with various Cork sides. Now living in Toronto, Eoin manages to learn a lot about his family history and pay tribute to his mother.

ACKNOWLEDGEMENTS

THIS BOOK WOULD never have come to pass if our readers didn't demand quality sportswriting every day. At a time where there's so much good journalism in our sports sections, online and in bookstore windows, we appreciate your time.

Last year's 'Behind The Lines' — our first volume — was a Hail Mary effort; but the punt paid off and people enjoyed the book. Thank you for the support.

As the hipster hurling fan says: there's a brother even better playing minor. If you liked the senior selection of stories between these covers, there's much more each day on our website *The42.ie* and the iOS and Android apps.

We're very fortunate to work alongside such a talented and dedicated group of people at Journal Media led by chief executive Adrián Acosta, who has driven on the idea of these books from the outset and keeps the lights on each day. As our friend Eddie O'Sullivan might say, thanks for the use of the hall.

Thanks to Susan Daly, *TheJournal.ie* editor, for the continued encouragement and support.

Thanks to Sinéad Casey and Kara Browning for their help and patience throughout the year, as well as Brian and Eamonn Fallon and Paul Kenny.

Graham Thew designed the cover and laid out the text with his typical style while Peter Bodkin, Christine Bohan, Michael

Freeman and Sinéad O'Carroll found themselves volunteered as the first readers and copy editors. Thank you all.

The42 team is not entirely represented here; Eoin Lúc Ó Ceallaigh produces incredible videos — some of them not about Carlow GAA — each day and his work deserves to be viewed on our YouTube channel. Thanks to messrs Chris O'Brien and Andrew Roberts for their work on our live shows and visual output throughout the year.

Jonathan Eig, who produced a hugely-impressive, doorstop biography of Muhammad Ali says of the pursuit of interview subjects: 'You don't try to get Michael Jordan in Chicago; wait til he's playing Sacramento on the road.'

Our team certainly got the job done away to The Kings; a quiet chat in a Cabra kitchen, a meeting on a bar terrace in Brisbane, a phone call punctuated by the sound of boarding calls and flight cancellation announcements. They're a talented group who, it's evident, love what they do.

Finally and most importantly, thanks to those sports people who were so generous with their time and trusted us to do their incredible personal stories some justice.

ADRIAN RUSSELL
Editor, The42